Contents

Module 3: The money side

Module 4: Global business

BUSINESS VOCABULARY in PRACTICE

Will Capel, Jamie Flockhart
& Sue Robbins

Collins

HarperCollins Publishers
77-85 Fulham Palace Road
Hammersmith
London W6 8JB

Third edition 2012

10 9 8 7 6 5 4 3

ISBN 978-0-00-742375-0

www.collinselt.com

A catalogue record for this book is available
from the British Library.

Typeset in India by Aptara

Printed in China by South China Printing Co. Ltd

Introduction

Targets and objectives

Welcome to *Business Vocabulary in Practice*, the book that gives you detailed explanations and thorough practice of the key business words, expressions and concepts you need to know for your business studies or in your working life.

To ensure that the language you learn is relevant for the workplace, the book uses example sentences from the Collins corpus. This is a constantly updated database of English language from a range of print and spoken sources. You can, therefore, be sure that any example used is an authentic use of English in a business context.

This book is for students at intermediate level or above, that is B1 to B2 on the Common European Framework of Reference.

Organisation of the material

Business Vocabulary in Practice contains 72 topics. Each topic is presented over two pages. You will find key vocabulary on the left-hand page and practice tasks on the right-hand page. We estimate that it should take you about 45 minutes to complete a topic.

The topics are organized into 15 different themes under four key areas of business. For more information on how the topics are organized, see the *Contents* page.

You will find answers to all the exercises in the answer key at the back of the book. This means that *Business Vocabulary in Practice* can be used either in the classroom or for self-study.

We hope you enjoy using this book and wish you the best of luck in your professional career.

Using the book

Left-hand pages: Key Vocabulary

On the left-hand pages you will find a short introduction followed by the key vocabulary for the topic, with an explanation in full of the meaning, example sentences using the vocabulary and other useful information.

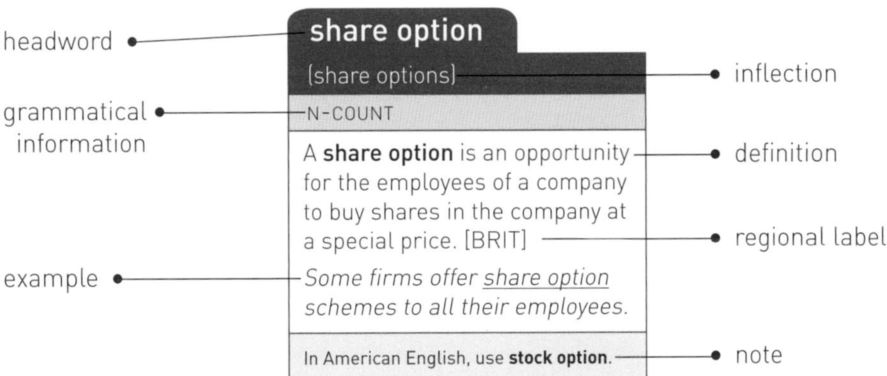

Headwords These have been carefully chosen to give you the language you'll need, whether you're studying business or using English at work. Each topic contains on average 8 key items of vocabulary, each presented in a clear and easy-to-understand way.

Grammatical information The entries also provide the key grammatical information you need to use the word properly. Noun plurals and verb inflections are given in brackets below the head-word, and the part of speech of the word is shown below this in small capitals. If the word can be used in different ways, the part of speech is shown on a new line inside the box.

For example, the word 'advertising' is always an uncountable noun, so it is shown like this:

advertising

N-UNCOUNT

Advertising is the activity of creating advertisements and making sure that people see them.
We offer digital marketing and Internet advertising technology and services.

while the word 'commute' can be a verb or a noun, so it is shown like this:

commute

(commutes, commuting, commuted)

VERB

If you **commute**, you travel a long distance every day between your home and your place of work.
She commutes to London every day.

N-COUNT

A **commute** is the journey that you make when you commute.
The average Los Angeles commute is over 60 miles a day.

The parts of speech used in this book are as follows:

ADJ
An **adjective** is used to tell you more about a person or thing; EG *sustainable; online*

ADV
An **adverb** gives more information about when, where, how or in what circumstances something happens; EG *in-house, freelance*

N-COUNT
A **count noun** has both singular and plural forms, and normally has a word such as 'a', 'an', 'the' or 'my' in front of it; EG *corporation/corporations; company/companies*

N-COUNT-COLL
A **countable collective noun** is a count noun which refers to a group of people or things. It behaves like a count noun, but when it is used in the singular form, it can be used with either a singular or a plural noun; EG *staff; works*

N-PLURAL
A **plural noun** is always plural, and is used with plural verbs; EG *overheads; economies of scale*

N-SING
A **singular noun** is always singular, and must have a word such as 'a', 'an', 'the' or 'my' in front of it; EG *public sector; world market*

N-UNCOUNT
An **uncount noun** has only one form, takes a singular verb and is not used with numbers or with 'a'; EG *diversification; flexitime*

N-VAR
A **variable noun** is a noun which can be used in both count and uncount forms; EG *recession, acquisition*

PHRASAL VERB
A **phrasal verb** is a combination of a verb and an adverb or a verb and a preposition, which together have a particular meaning; EG *power ahead; turn around*

PHRASE
A **phrase** is a group of words which have a particular meaning when they are used together. This meaning is not always understandable from the separate parts; EG *under licence; go out of business*

VERB
A **verb** is a word which is used to say what someone or something does or what happens to them, or to give information about them; EG *download, merge*

Definitions All of the definitions are written in full sentences in simple, natural English. This allows us to show you the typical patterns and grammatical behaviour of a word, as well as the meaning.

Labels Almost all of the terms in this book are used in all varieties of English. If a term is used only in British English, we have added the label [BRIT] after the definition. If it is mostly used in British English, but is sometimes used in other varieties, we have added the label [mainly BRIT].

Examples Each headword and definition is followed by an example. All of the examples are taken from the Collins Corpus, a huge database of real language from a variety of sources. The examples have been carefully chosen to show common patterns and typical uses of the word or phrase, so that you can see how it is really used in English today.

Notes Notes give you extra information relating to an entry, for example a related word or phrase, or a word or phrase which has the same meaning as the headword.

Collocation boxes These boxes present a main word or phrase, and show you other words or structures (collocations) which are regularly used with the main word or phrase.

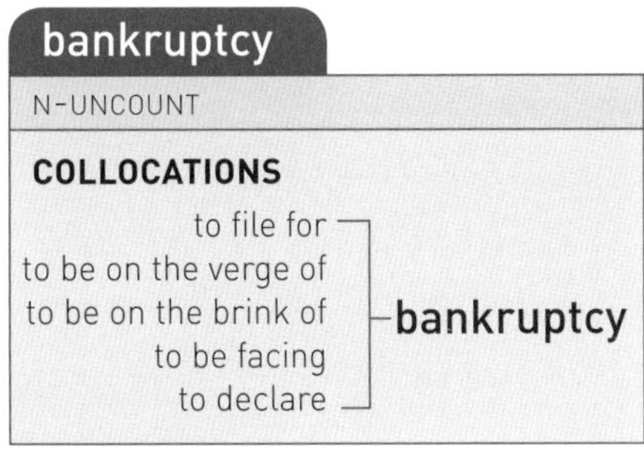

Information boxes On some left-hand pages, you'll find Information boxes. These give you more information about the topic.

'See also' boxes Below the introduction on some left-hand pages you will find a box marked 'See also'. This contains cross-references to other topics in the book, where you can find explanations and examples of other useful words related to the topic you are studying. 'See also' boxes look like this:

See also			
Topic 7.4	**stakeholder**	Topic 11.1	**cash flow**

Right-hand pages: Practice Tasks

The right-hand pages contain a variety of tasks designed to help you practise all the vocabulary from the left-hand pages.

Exercises Exercise types include: fill the gaps exercises; matching exercises; completing diagrams and tables; true/false questions and multiple-choice exercises. You will find answers to all the exercises in the answer key at the back of the book.

Mini Webquests In addition to the exercises on the right-hand page, there are short *Mini Webquests*, which suggest further areas of research, should you wish to look into the topic in more depth.

Reflections Some right-hand pages have a short *Reflection* task. These contain one or more questions designed to make you think about your own experience and knowledge in relation to the topic.

Index

At the back of the book you will find an index, which contains all the words and phrases that are defined or presented with collocations on the left-hand pages. This will allow you to find the explanation of a particular term quickly and easily.

Module 1 The product life cycle

The product life cycle is the sequence of events in the history of a service or product from its development and launch to its withdrawal from the market.

The way a particular service or product is received and used by the customer will usually inform future research and development.

Topic 1 Research and development

1.1 Market research
1.2 Product development
1.3 Testing
1.4 Inventions, patenting and intellectual property rights

Topic 2 Production

2.1 Types of production
2.2 Sourcing
2.3 Quality control
2.4 Outsourcing
2.5 Working in production

Topic 3 Marketing

3.1 The marketing mix
3.2 Promotion
3.3 Price, packaging and place
3.4 Branding
3.5 Marketing strategies

Topic 4 Sales

4.1 What makes a good salesperson?
4.2 Orders and stock control
4.3 Distribution
4.4 Sales methods
4.5 Retailing

Topic 5 Customer service

5.1 Customer care
5.2 Customer feedback
5.3 Customer relationship management
5.4 Customer reviews
5.5 Consumer protection

TOPIC 1.1 Market research

Market research is the activity of collecting and studying information about what people want, need and buy. This information can be gathered in different ways.

qualitative

ADJ

Qualitative market research involves individuals or small groups of people (called 'focus groups') being interviewed to find out their beliefs, values and opinions.

Our emphasis was much more on qualitative research than statistical analysis.

focus group

(focus groups)

N-COUNT

A **focus group** is a specially selected group of people who are intended to represent the general public. **Focus groups** have discussions in which their opinions are recorded as a form of market research.

Our research findings are based on four focus groups, each of up to eight people.

quantitative

ADJ

Quantitative market research involves large groups of people giving information (for example through questionnaires) in order to create statistics.

The survey was set up to record masses of quantitative data, as well as qualitative data in the form of written comments.

market research

N-UNCOUNT

COLLOCATIONS

to conduct / to do / to carry out — market research

primary data

N-UNCOUNT

Primary data is information that is collected at first-hand, for example in interviews.

The report doesn't contain any primary data or provide deep analysis.

Primary data is collected through **field research**.

information

N-UNCOUNT

COLLOCATIONS

to gather / to collect / to obtain / to supply / to share / to disclose — information

secondary data

N-UNCOUNT

Secondary data is information about a subject that has already been written or published.

Sources of secondary data can be internal, such as sales records or customer feedback forms.

Secondary data is collected through **desk research**.

field research

N-UNCOUNT

Field research is research that is done in a real, natural environment, for example by interviewing people, rather than in a theoretical way.

Field research provides access to primary information, through direct contact with consumers.

desk research

N-UNCOUNT

Desk research is research that is done in a theoretical way, by reading what has already been written about a subject.

Desk research is where the researcher uses information from sources such as books and sales reports.

TASKS

Exercise 1

Use the terms in the box to complete the paragraph.

primary	*quantitative*	*questionnaires*	*interviews*	*qualitative*
market research	*focus groups*	*secondary*	*desk*	*field*

(a)________________ is the gathering of information about what consumers want and need, and what makes them buy. **(b)**________________ market research involves small groups of people, for example using **(c)**________________, while **(d)**________________ market research involves large groups of people, for example using surveys or **(e)**________________. **(f)**________________ data is collected through the use of surveys, (i.e. questioning individuals) or **(g)**________________, (i.e. questioning groups of people, for example). This kind of data is collected through **(h)**________________ research. **(i)**________________ data includes information from sources such as the media or trade associations. Such data is collected through **(j)**________________ research.

Exercise 2

Which of the following are examples of primary data and which are examples of secondary data?

	Primary	Secondary
1. published sales figures	☐	☐
2. company invoices	☐	☐
3. information published by another company	☐	☐
4. data from telephone interviews	☐	☐
5. data from online polls	☐	☐
6. focus groups	☐	☐

Exercise 3

Match the two halves of the sentences.

1. Market research is the process of	**a.** asking questions of respondents, either by filling in a questionnaire or by interview.
2. Primary data is information which	**b.** are an example of qualitative market research.
3. Secondary data is information which	**c.** produces data which can be statistically analysed.
4. Carrying out a survey involves	**d.** is already available, both inside and outside the organization.
5. Interviews with individuals	**e.** no-one has yet collected.
6. Quantitative market research	**f.** finding out what customers want and need, and what makes them buy.

Reflection

Have you ever conducted a focus group or written a questionnaire for customers? What skills do you think you need to have for these two market research activities?

TOPIC 1.2 Product development

Product development is the process of bringing a new product to the market place.

product-led

ADJ

A company that is **product-led** aims to develop new products and then create a market for them.

A switch from product-led to consumer-led marketing gives an in-built advantage to small, flexible companies.

customize

(customizes, customizing, customized)

VERB

If you **customize** something, you change its appearance or features to suit your tastes or needs.

This control allows photographers to customize the camera's basic settings.

market sector

(market sectors)

N-COUNT

A **market sector** is one part of a market, consisting of related products or services.

It achieved this growth by identifying a market sector, and moving quickly to become the market leader in that sector.

customer-led

ADJ

A company that is **customer-led** develops new products based on market research, which tells them what customers want.

We have a customer-led marketing strategy.

product development

N-VAR

COLLOCATIONS

(a) new / (an) innovative / (an) effective / next-generation **product development**

approach

(approaches)

N-COUNT

Your **approach** to a task, problem or situation is the way that you deal with it or think about it.

They are now adopting a much more aggressive approach to marketing their product.

CAD

N-UNCOUNT

CAD is the use of computer software in the design of things such as cars, buildings and machines. **CAD** is an abbreviation for 'computer-aided design'.

The introduction of 3D CAD capabilities was identified as the most important operational goal.

reverse engineering

N-UNCOUNT

Reverse engineering is a process in which a product or system is analysed in order to see how it works, so that a similar version of the product or system can be produced more cheaply.

Through reverse engineering, the company was able to make drugs still on patent internationally, and to sell them at a tenth of the international price.

R&D

N-UNCOUNT

R&D is the part of a company's activity that is concerned with applying the results of scientific research to develop new products and improve existing ones. **R&D** is an abbreviation for 'research and development'.

Companies that spend a lot of money on research and development tend to be the most successful.

TASKS

Exercise 1

Use the terms in the box to complete the paragraph.

reverse engineering	*market sector*	*product*	*R & D*
existing product	*product-led*	*CAD*	*customize*

New product ideas can be generated by market research in a customer-led approach. A **(a)**____________________ approach is where a company develops a product, possibly as a result of technical innovation, before there is a market for the **(b)**____________________. **(c)**____________________ allows engineers and designers to create 2D (two dimensional) plans and 3D (three dimensional) visualizations for new products. **(d)**____________________ is the process where a company takes an **(e)**____________________ and analyses it to see how it works so that a similar version can be produced more cheaply. One recent trend has been the ability of consumers to **(f)**____________________ a product to suit their needs. How much companies reinvest their profits in the **(g)**____________________ of new products will depend on the competitive environment of their **(h)**____________________.

Exercise 2

Match each sentence on the left with the sentence which follows it on the right.

1. In our company all the employees are encouraged to contribute ideas for new products.	**a.** This reverse engineering can be very enlightening.
2. For a long time we used more traditional methods of product development.	**b.** Some very good ideas have come out of this staff suggestion scheme.
3. Our research department often dismantles our competitors' latest products to see how they are built.	**c.** Most of our merchandise is very expensive.
4. We develop new products in our laboratories and then research the market to find out how to sell them.	**d.** Now we use CAD a lot more.
5. We are a large department store that sells luxury goods.	**e.** We adopt a product-led approach.

Exercise 3

Match each phrase on the left with an example of it on the right.

1. reverse engineering	**a.** the first television sets of the 20th century are introduced
2. a customized product	**b.** patented pharmaceuticals are analysed, made generically and sold at a fraction of the price of the original patented drug
3. research and development	**c.** a car with a choice of colours, interior materials and extras as part of the basic specification
4. a product-led approach	**d.** manufacturers invest around 4% of their sales turnover in this while pharmaceutical companies will spend between 15 and 20%

Mini Webquest

- Technological advances often allow manufacturers to create new products, for example multimedia devices or games consoles. Look online for a product which was developed using this kind of product-led approach.

TOPIC 1.3 Testing

Product testing involves, on the one hand, testing that the product is suitable for its intended market and, on the other hand, making sure that the product functions as planned and is safe to use.

market test

(market tests, market testing, market tested)

N-COUNT

If a company carries out a **market test**, it asks a group of people to try a new product or service and give their opinions on it.

The new product performed well in a market test in Las Vegas.

VERB

If a company **market tests** a new product or service, a group of people are asked to try it and are then asked for their opinions on it.

These nuts have been market tested and found to be most suited to the Australian palate.

suitable

ADJ

Something that is **suitable** for a particular purpose or occasion is right or acceptable for it.

Some experts now say the product is only suitable for a very limited market.

test

N-COUNT

COLLOCATIONS

to pass a / to fail a / to undergo a / to perform a / to administer a / to conduct a — test

test market

(test markets, test marketing, test marketed)

N-COUNT

A **test market** is a geographical area or a group of people that tries a new product or service so that its qualities can be evaluated.

Four of America's top five test markets for new products are in the state of Wisconsin.

VERB

If a company **test markets** a new product or service, a group of people are asked to try it and are then asked for their opinions on it.

They will test market a new line of bottled water in the West early next year.

pilot

(pilots)

N-COUNT

A **pilot** is a scheme or project which is used to test an idea before deciding whether to introduce it on a larger scale.

The service is being expanded following the success of a pilot scheme.

A pilot can also be called a **pilot scheme** or a **pilot project**.

launch

(launches, launching, launched)

VERB

If a company **launches** a new product, it makes it available to the public.

In launching a new product overseas a firm has open to it many pricing options.

N-COUNT

The **launch** of a new product is the act of making it available to the public.

This is the most important product launch from Microsoft in six years.

modify

(modifies, modifying, modified)

VERB

If you **modify** something, you change it slightly, usually in order to improve it.

Prototypes have to be built, tested and modified in the light of experience, and only then put into production.

TASKS

Exercise 1

Use the terms in the box to complete each sentence.

test market	*passed*	*pilot*
modified	*market tests*	*fail*

1. Last year we conducted 28,000 ________________ on 6,000 different product combinations.
2. We've decided to ________________ the device next month.
3. The drug will be put on the market after it has ________________ its safety tests.
4. We think that the government should make public the lists of all products that are genetically ________________.
5. ________________ studies are carried out before a drug can be sold to the public.
6. They will ban products which ________________ government safety tests.

Exercise 2

Did the following products or services prove suitable (S) or unsuitable (U) for the test market?

1. 80% of those questioned said they enjoyed the drink.
2. 33% said they would use the service again in future.
3. 90% did not feel the product offered value for money.
4. 75% of those asked said they'd had a very positive experience of the service.
5. The majority of those questioned said they'd never buy the product again.

Exercise 3

Match the examples with the correct term.

1. We initially launched the product in just one region, before going national.	**a.** pilot study
2. We found that these were the best cities for generating useful market data.	**b.** modifications
3. The drugs are currently being tested by a small group of people.	**c.** market test
4. We expect to make several changes to the service before it is launched internationally.	**d.** test markets

Mini Webquest

- Find out why the Mercedes A-Class car had to be modified after a Swedish market test in 1997.

TOPIC 1.4 Inventions, patenting and intellectual property rights

Companies protect their inventions and intellectual property rights by patenting and copyrighting them.

See also	
Topic 13.3	**user license, site license**

invention

(inventions)

N-COUNT

If you invent something such as a machine or process, you are the first person to think of it or make it. An **invention** is a machine, device or system that has been invented by someone.

The company is planning to market the invention to a wide range of advertisers.

N-UNCOUNT

Invention is the act of inventing something that has never been made or used before.

Its origins are linked to the invention of the first electronic computers.

patent

(patents, patenting, patented)

N-COUNT

A **patent** is an official right to be the only person or company allowed to make or sell a new product for a certain period of time.

He applied for a patent on his invention.

VERB

If you **patent** something, you obtain a patent for it.

A British firm has patented a technological aid to keep airline pilots awake.

under licence

PHRASE

If someone does something **under licence**, they do it by special permission from a government or other authority.

We decided to have it made by another company under licence to increase capacity.

patent

N-COUNT

COLLOCATIONS

to file a / to grant somebody a / to have a / to apply for a — **patent on/for *something***

piracy

N-UNCOUNT

COLLOCATIONS

software / Internet / music / to prevent / to combat / to fight — **piracy**

copyright

(copyrights)

N-VAR

If someone has **copyright** on something, such as a photo, a map, or a piece of writing, music, or software, it is illegal to reproduce or distribute it without their permission.

Owning the copyright to digital images will give the gallery some protection under the law.

We will file charges against anyone for breaching copyright.

piracy

N-UNCOUNT

You can refer to the illegal copying of things such as DVDs, downloads or computer programs as **piracy**.

The maximum prison sentence for software piracy is 10 years.

intellectual property rights

N-PLURAL

If someone has the **intellectual property rights** to an idea or invention, they are legally allowed to develop the idea or invention, and nobody else can do so without their permission.

The aim is to protect intellectual property rights from abuse by pirates or patent-holders.

TASKS

Exercise 1

Use the terms in the box to complete the paragraph.

patenting	*invention*	*piracy*
copyrighted	*under licence*	*intellectual property rights*

(a)___________________ is the creation of totally new products or production techniques through a process of innovation. Inventors protect their inventions by **(b)**___________________ them. Others may be permitted to use ideas for which there is a patent if they pay a royalty. They are then said to use the invention **(c)**___________________. If a person owns the **(d)**___________________ to an invention, they have the right to develop it. **(e)**___________________ is the illegal copying and use of **(f)**___________________ material, for example through illegal downloads or file sharing.

Exercise 2

Match each sentence on the left with the sentence which follows it on the right.

1. Our research department recently developed a new computer programme used to guide the production robots in the factory.	**a.** Making products under licence like this has been very good for our firm.
2. We recently installed new computers in our factory. We bought the most sophisticated equipment available.	**b.** These patents are essential to modern medicine.
3. Our bottling and soft drinks plant is the only one in the region that can legally make Cool Cola.	**c.** We are really at the leading edge of design.
4. Our company's head of R&D was sacked last year after the company was prosecuted for copying a new idea from one of our rivals.	**d.** The machines use state-of-the-art technology.
5. R&D is very expensive in the pharmaceutical industry, so our legal department gets full protection for our new developments.	**e.** The head of the legal department should have advised him that the company was infringing a patent.
6. We are a small company that specializes in designing computer programmes for the print business. We employ some of the best technicians in the country.	**f.** After manufacturing the software we kept the intellectual property rights to it.

Exercise 3

Match the two halves of the sentences.

1. The government want to update copyright protection	**a.** a device that demands a code before pilots can operate the controls.
2. Almost every major music release this year	**b.** technological inventions across Europe.
3. The air safety consultant has patented	**c.** to combat software piracy.
4. The new law is focused on protecting	**d.** has encountered the problem of Internet piracy.

Reflection

Why do you think copyrighting and patenting are important to companies?
Have you ever had to deal with copyright issues in your work?

TOPIC 2.1 Types of production

Methods of production differ according to the number and types of products required, the level of investment possible and the technology available.

See also

Topic 2.5 — **production line**

one-off production

N-UNCOUNT

One-off production is the activity of making unique products. These products are often made by someone who has special skill and training. Examples of products made in this way are a piece of jewellery or a specially commissioned wedding dress.

We've spoken to a craftsman who specialises in one-off production.

batch production

N-UNCOUNT

Batch production is the activity of making similar products together in stages. Examples of products made in this way are loaves of bread or office furniture.

Parry Confectionery has moved from a batch production system to a flow-production one.

mass production

N-UNCOUNT

Mass production is the activity of making a large number of products that are all the same on an assembly line or a production line. Examples of products made in this way are motor cars and engines.

Cars as well as small consumer goods such as chocolate bars are produced by mass production.

Mass production can also be called **flow production**.

just-in-time

N-UNCOUNT

Just-in-time is a manufacturing method which aims to reduce wastage by keeping stocks low and by producing goods only when they are required. The abbreviation **JIT** is also used.

Just-in-time has allowed firms to reduce the level of stocks they keep.

You can also talk about **just-in-time manufacturing**, or **just-in-time production**.

lean

ADJ

Lean manufacturing and **lean** production are manufacturing methods which aim to reduce wastage, for example by keeping stocks low and by working more flexibly.

They introduced efficiency-raising techniques such as lean manufacturing.

production

N-UNCOUNT

COLLOCATIONS

ready for / to be in / to go into / to go out of — **production**

plant

(plants)

N-COUNT

A **plant** is a factory or a place where power is produced.

The plant provides forty per cent of the country's electricity.

works

N-COUNT-COLL

A **works** is a place where something is manufactured or where an industrial process is carried out.

Works is used to refer to one or to more than one of these places.

The steel works, one of the landmarks of Stoke-on-Trent, could be seen for miles.

I always eat in the works canteen.

factory

(factories)

N-COUNT

A **factory** is a large building where machines are used to make large quantities of goods.

He owned furniture factories in New York State.

TASKS

Exercise 1

Use the terms in the box to complete the paragraph.

factory	*production process*	*lean production*	*production*	*just-in-time*

If companies adopt lean manufacturing or **(a)**__________________ techniques, they are interested in making the **(b)**__________________ more efficient. They try to keep all inputs to the process to a minimum. This could mean using the fewest workers they can, cutting down on the amount of raw materials needed, or using as little **(c)**__________________ space as possible, for example. One of the operations that is central to lean manufacturing is **(d)**__________________ production. This manufacturing method aims to reduce costs by keeping stocks low. Instead of keeping stocks in the warehouse, the company asks its suppliers to make frequent deliveries so that they can be used straight away. **(e)**__________________ can then exactly match the amount of goods required, so that the company does not incur costs on warehousing finished goods.

Exercise 2

Which term is the odd one out in each line?

1. manufacturing factory production
2. plant manufacturer factory
3. works manufacturing facility output
4. output producer manufacturer
5. produce manufacture works

Exercise 3

Are the sentences ***true*** *or* ***false****?*

	True	False
a. One-off production is used to manufacture a large number of similar products.	☐	☐
b. Batch production involves making similar products together in stages.	☐	☐
c. A company using lean production techniques is likely to have a large warehouse full of finished products.	☐	☐
d. The JIT manufacturing system is a part of the lean production approach.	☐	☐
e. Car production is usually carried out at a plant.	☐	☐

Exercise 4

Fine Field, a company which manufactures garden tools, uses the JIT system of manufacturing. What do you know about the following, therefore?

a. The amount of stock Fine Field hold

b. The amount of space available in their factory

c. Bulk buying (buying in very large quantities)

d. The costs of holding stock in their warehouse

Mini Webquest

- Find out about the origins of JIT.

TOPIC

2.2

Sourcing

Those involved in production need to source raw materials and components for the manufacturing of their products.

supplier

(suppliers)

N-COUNT

A **supplier** is a person, company or organization that sells or supplies something such as goods or equipment to customers.

They will switch suppliers if foreign manufacturers are more efficient.

tender

(tenders, tendering, tendered)

N-VAR

A **tender** is a formal offer to supply goods or to do a particular job, and a statement of the price that you or your company will charge. If a contract is put out to **tender**, formal offers are invited. If a company wins a **tender**, their offer is accepted.

The company won a competitive tender for the contract.

VERB

If a company **tenders** for something, it makes a formal offer to supply goods or do a job for a particular price.

The company is tendering for a contract to replace the boundary fences on the site.

source

(sources, sourcing, sourced)

VERB

If a person or firm **sources** a product or a raw material, they find someone who will supply it.

Sourcing the best raw materials is an important first step in ensuring a high quality product.

source

VERB

COLLOCATIONS

to source – components / materials / equipment / goods / suppliers

sourcing

N-UNCOUNT

COLLOCATIONS

local / offshore / overseas / global / strategic – sourcing

component

(components)

N-COUNT

The **components** of something are the parts that it is made of.

As component costs come down, PC prices come down.

You can also use **component part**.

raw materials

N-PLURAL

Raw materials are materials that are in their natural state, before they are processed or used in manufacturing.

We import raw materials such as raw cotton, wool and silk, and convert them into basic manufactured products for export.

futures

N-PLURAL

When people trade in **futures**, they buy commodities or raw materials, such as coffee or oil, or foreign currency at a price that is agreed at the time of purchase for items which are delivered sometime in the future.

This report could spur some buying in corn futures when the market opens today.

TASKS

Exercise 1

Use the terms in the box to complete the paragraph.

futures	*tender*	*components*	*sourced*
product	*raw materials*	*suppliers*	*manufacturers*

Manufacturers will often use the **(a)**____________________ markets to secure the price of **(b)**____________________, for example aluminium, steel and cobalt, which they will require for production at a point in the future. When looking to source **(c)**____________________, manufacturers will ask potential **(d)**____________________ to **(e)**____________________ for the contract. Raw materials may be **(f)**____________________ locally or overseas. Software programs from companies like SAP and Oracle allow **(g)**____________________ to pick components when assembling the finished **(h)**____________________.

Exercise 2

Look at the following table of suppliers who are tendering for a contract to supply goods to Perini, a company based in Italy.

Supplier	Location	Price offered	Delivery time
A&M	UK	1 dollar per unit	1 month
Kressler	Switzerland	0.5 dollars per unit	6 months
Zhang Ltd	China	0.3 dollars per unit	8 months

1. Which supplier is offering the lowest tender?
2. Which supplier is offering the highest tender?
3. Which supplier can offer the fastest delivery time?
4. How many suppliers are based overseas?
5. If Perini require the goods within the next seven months, who is most likely to win the tender?

Exercise 3

Match the raw materials on the left with the correct product on the right.

1. aluminium	**a.** gloves
2. coffee	**b.** jet fuel
3. cotton	**c.** jeans
4. oil	**d.** soft drinks cans
5. latex	**e.** espresso

Reflection

What are the raw materials or components that your company (or one you know well) has to source to make its products?
What are the issues attached to sourcing these things, for example delivery times or quality assurance?

Mini Webquest

- Find out as much as you can about the Kanban system.
- Find out about the concept of a reverse auction.

TOPIC 2.3 Quality control

Quality control (QC), or quality assurance (QA) is about making sure that goods or services are "fit for purpose", that is of an acceptable standard to the consumer.

quality circle
(quality circles)

N-COUNT

A **quality circle** is a small group of workers and managers who meet to solve problems and improve the quality of the organization's products or services.

A team approach means closer collaboration between managers and workers and among workers in quality circles.

benchmarking

N-UNCOUNT

Benchmarking is a process in which a company compares its products and methods with those of the most successful companies in its field, in order to try to improve its own performance.

We conducted an extensive benchmarking of best practices and restructured our activities accordingly.

TQM

N-UNCOUNT

TQM is a set of management principles aimed at improving performance throughout a company, especially by involving employees in decision-making. **TQM** is an abbreviation for 'total quality management'.

TQM is a way of bringng everyone into the processes of improvement.

quality

N-UNCOUNT

COLLOCATIONS

quality – control / assurance / improvement / management

monitor
(monitors, monitoring, monitored)

VERB

If you **monitor** something, you regularly check its development or progress, and sometimes comment on it.

His progress is monitored under a personal development plan.

inspect
(inspects, inspecting, inspected)

VERB

When officials **inspect** a place or a group of people, they visit the place or people and make careful checks, for example in order to find out whether regulations are being obeyed.

Each hotel is inspected and, if it fulfils certain criteria, is recommended.

routine check
(routine checks)

N-COUNT

If someone carries out a **routine check** on a product, place or piece of equipment, they examine it as part of a regular checking procedure in order to see if there are any problems with it.

We can view the information held on the database at any time and make routine checks.

Six Sigma is a well-known system developed by *Motorola* in the 1970s for improving quality and minimizing defects or errors in manufacturing processes.

Six Sigma is a statistical term to measure how far a given process deviates from perfection.

TASKS

Exercise 1

Choose one of the terms in the box to complete each definition.

total quality management (TQM)	*benchmarking*	*monitor*
quality control/quality assurance	*routine checks*	

a. The collection of management techniques known as ______________ aims to improve the company's performance, and is based on the principle that it is cheaper in the long term to do the job right the first time round, rather than making mistakes and fixing them afterwards.

b. Companies using TQM believe that quality is the responsibility of every department and every worker. This is very different from the traditional view in which ______________ is a process in the chain of production, and is the sole responsibility of a quality controller. He or she may carry out ______________ and inspections.

c. Many companies consult their customers about their views on quality, and use market research to find out what their customers think. This kind of consultation forms part of the ______________ process.

d. We feel that it's important to ______________ the progress of all employees in the company, so we have regular reviews and appraisals.

e. ______________ is the practice of comparing business practices between companies.

Exercise 2

Match each statement on the left with one on the right.

1. Our company is starting a quality assurance programme.	**a.** We will be examining the leading competitor in our field and trying to meet or improve on their standards.
2. Our R&D department will adopt a benchmarking strategy.	**b.** We will get members of staff to meet and resolve problems that we have with particular products.
3. We will set up quality circles.	**c.** We will be focusing on quality with a view to increasing our effectiveness, flexibility and competitiveness.
4. We will take a total quality management approach.	**d.** We hope to involve all employees in making decisions about quality control.

Exercise 3

When assessing the quality of a product, which of these factors should be considered?

1. physical appearance	**3.** reliability	**5.** image	**7.** suitability
2. after-sales service	**4.** durability	**6.** reputation	**8.** price

Exercise 4

The following are all quality control techniques. Which ones are features of traditional quality control (QC) and which ones are specific to total quality management (TQM)? Tick (✓) the appropriate column.

	QC	TQM
a. making everyone in the company take responsibility for quality	☐	☐
b. making quality the responsibility of the quality control department	☐	☐
c. constant monitoring and routine checks of the whole business	☐	☐
d. using a quality controller to check finished work for defects	☐	☐
e. the use of quality circles to generate discussion about the cause of quality problems and their solutions	☐	☐
f. being committed to one's customers and knowing about their needs and expectations	☐	☐
g. assuming customers are happy unless they complain about the quality of goods	☐	☐

Mini Webquest

- Find out more about TQM and Six Sigma. Which came first?

TOPIC 2.4 Outsourcing

Outsourcing is the term given to situations where manufacturers will sub-contract production to a third party, often in a foreign country.

subcontract

(subcontracts, subcontracting, subcontracted)

VERB

If one firm **subcontracts** part of its work to another firm, it pays the other firm to do part of the work that it has been employed to do.

They cut costs by subcontracting work out to other local firms.

outsource

(outsources, outsourcing, outsourced)

VERB

If a company **outsources** goods or services, it pays workers from outside the company to supply the goods or provide the services

Increasingly, corporate clients are seeking to outsource the management of their facilities.

core business

N-UNCOUNT

The **core business** of a company is the most important or most profitable area of its activity.

We decided to expand our core business in overseas markets.

outsource

VERB

COLLOCATIONS

to outsource work / services / tasks / management / activities / manufacturing

lead time

(lead times)

N-COUNT

Lead time is the time between the original design or idea for a particular product and its actual production.

They aim to cut production lead times to under 18 months.

third party

(third parties)

N-COUNT

A **third party** is a person or organization that is not one of the two main people or organizations involved in a business agreement.

We have to rely on third parties for customer support.

production

N-UNCOUNT

COLLOCATIONS

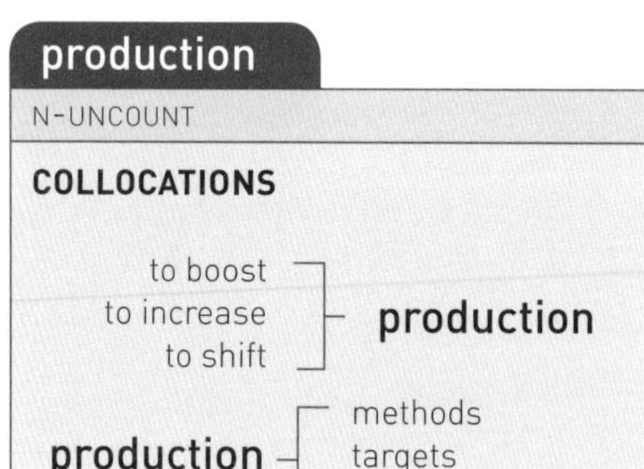

to boost / to increase / to shift **production**

production methods / targets / costs

overseas

ADJ

You use **overseas** to describe things that involve or are in foreign countries, usually across a sea or an ocean.

How active is the company in overseas markets?

Reasons for outsourcing:

- to reduce costs, for example by using cheaper labour
- to increase production
- to improve quality
- to reduce production and delivery lead times to market
- to enable the manufacturer to focus on their core business

TASKS

Exercise 1

Use the terms in the box to complete the paragraph.

core business	*production*	*quality*	*relocate*	*subcontracting*
third party	*increase*	*firms*	*overseas*	*outsource*

Many businesses **(a)**________________ all or part of their **(b)**________________ to another company, either locally or **(c)**________________. By moving their production to a **(d)**________________, many **(e)**________________ are able to spend more time on their **(f)**________________. Another advantage of outsourcing is that it allows a company to **(g)**________________ production, while at the same time reducing production costs. In addition, by **(h)**________________ work outside the company, the **(i)**________________ of production may also be improved. This is why so many manufacturers choose to **(j)**________________ their production overseas.

Exercise 2

Read the article below and then say whether the following sentences are true or false.

In 2002 James Dyson made 800 semi-skilled UK workers redundant at his UK factory and relocated production of his innovative vacuum cleaners to Malaysia.

There was no reduction in the quality of the vacuum cleaners and indeed James Dyson claimed quality had improved by moving to Malaysia.

Production costs fell by 30% and the subsequent increase in profitability of his company allowed him to invest more in his research division in the UK and to employ more highly trained research scientists there.

1. James Dyson relocated production to the UK.

2. Moving production led to a reduction in quality of the vacuum cleaners.

3. Production costs were reduced, allowing Dyson to spend more on research.

4. Several hundred workers were made redundant as a result of outsourcing.

5. Dyson's research division is based in Malaysia.

Exercise 3

Match the two halves of the sentences.

1. Outsourcing is when a	**a.** they can reduce their delivery lead time to market.
2. Subcontracting work to another firm	**b.** manufacturer subcontracts production to a third party.
3. If a company outsources,	**c.** can help to reduce production costs.

Reflection

Have you ever worked for a company that outsourced part or all of its production?
Can you think of any disadvantages to outsourcing?

TOPIC 2.5

Working in production

The role of people in manufacturing has changed a lot with the introduction of automation and the use of robots in methods of production.

automation

N-UNCOUNT

Automation refers to the use of machines to do work that was previously done by people.

Tremendous progress has been made in factory automation by using robots.

blue-collar

ADJ

Blue-collar workers work in industry, doing physical work, rather than in offices.

The average CEO makes 411 times the salaries of their blue-collar workers.

job satisfaction

N-UNCOUNT

Job satisfaction is the pleasure that you get from doing your job.

Employees can benefit from reduced commuting time, more flexible work hours and increased job satisfaction.

robot

(robots)

N-COUNT

A **robot** is a machine which is programmed to move and perform certain tasks automatically.

At the factory in Japan, the cars are assembled largely by robots.

worker

N-COUNT

COLLOCATIONS

a skilled / a semi-skilled / an unskilled / a manual / a blue-collar / a white-collar / a clerical — **worker**

team

N-COUNT

COLLOCATIONS

to join a / to build a / to lead a / to work in a / to work as a / to work as part of a — **team**

teamwork

N-UNCOUNT

Teamwork is the ability that a group of people have to work well together.

Even in jobs not requiring teamwork, relationships with co-workers, supervisors or clients can be stressful.

production line

(production lines)

N-COUNT

A **production line** is an arrangement of machines in a factory where the products pass from machine to machine until they are finished.

It should be recognized that we are not robots in a production line.

white-collar

ADJ

White-collar workers work in offices rather than doing physical work.

Companies are moving thousands of white-collar jobs to developing countries.

job rotation

N-UNCOUNT

Job rotation is a system which allows a team of workers to move around a production line, dealing with all parts of a product until it is finished, rather than dealing with only one part of the product repeatedly.

Job rotation results in a more flexible workforce, which may be useful at holiday time or when employees are off sick.

TASKS

Exercise 1

Use the terms in the box to complete the paragraph.

job rotation	*production line*	*automation*
teams	*robots*	*job satisfaction*

Products such as cars are made on a **(a)**__________________. Many of the tasks previously carried out by workers have been taken over by **(b)**__________________ – part of the process of **(c)**__________________. Working on a production line can be very repetitive, so companies try to find ways to improve **(d)**__________________, while maintaining high quality levels. **(e)**__________________ is a system that allows people to move around the production line, doing different jobs. Rather than carrying out one function repetitively, workers are put into **(f)**__________________ and carry out all the functions to complete production.

Exercise 2

Which jobs are held by blue-collar workers and which are held by white-collar workers? Complete the table.

1. technical support adviser
2. plumber
3. washing machine repairman
4. recruitment consultant
5. receptionist
6. web designer
7. builder
8. electrician
9. teacher
10. architect
11. delivery van driver
12. lawyer

Blue-collar	White-collar

Exercise 3

Match the two halves of each sentence.

1. A team is often defined as	**a.** a clerical worker in a municipal office.
2. Last year, she retired from her job as	**b.** have helped to relieve local labour-market shortages.
3. One result of automation is	**c.** a group of people brought together to achieve a particular objective.
4. Foreign computer programmers, health professionals and other skilled workers	**d.** greatly increased flexibility in the production process.

Reflection

What are the benefits of automation?
How important is job satisfaction to you?

TOPIC 3.1 The marketing mix

People talk about *the four Ps* in the marketing mix: price, promotion, place and product.

See also
Topic 3.2 **advertising**
Topic 4.3 **distribution chain**

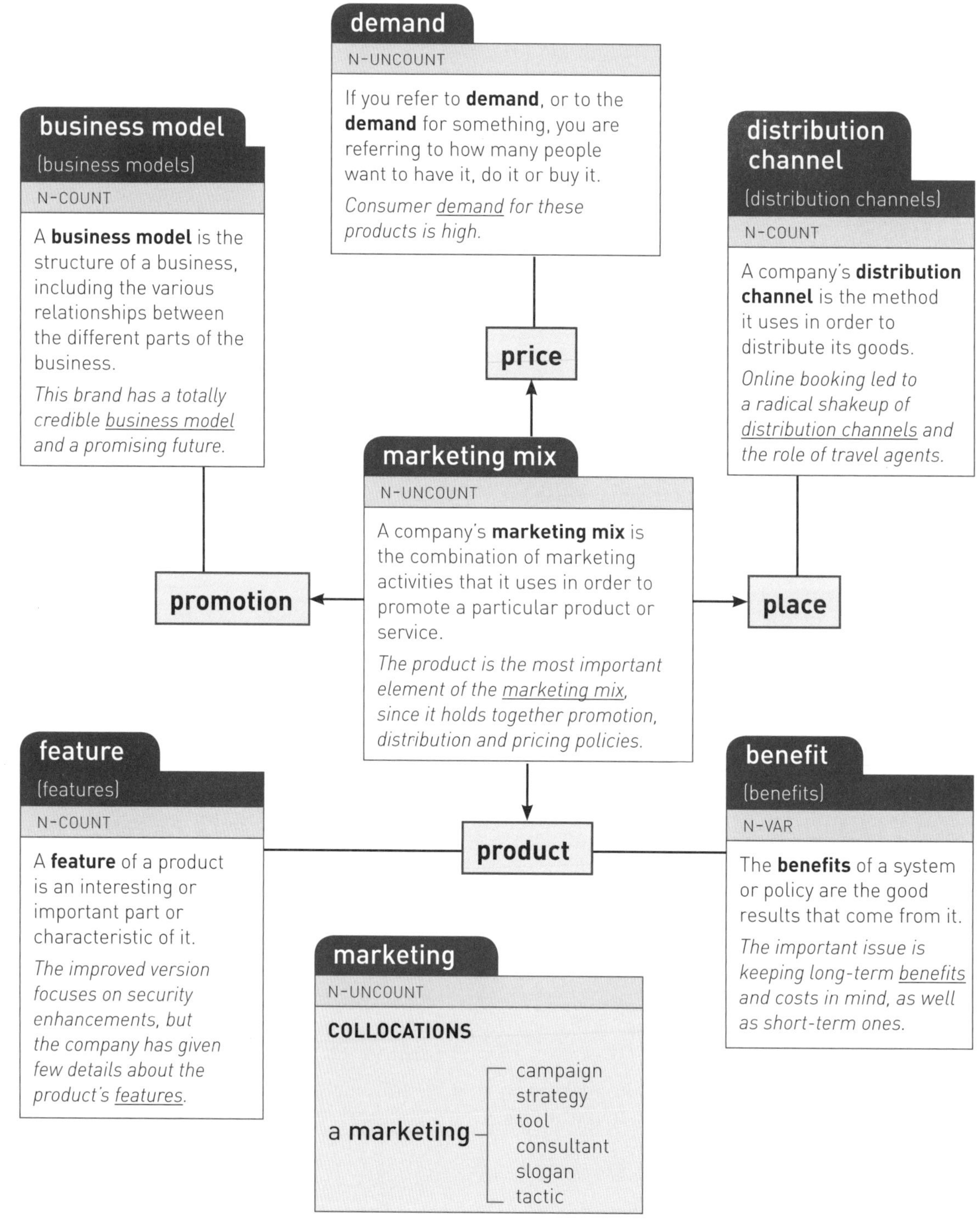

demand
N-UNCOUNT
If you refer to **demand**, or to the **demand** for something, you are referring to how many people want to have it, do it or buy it.
Consumer <u>demand</u> for these products is high.

business model
(business models)
N-COUNT
A **business model** is the structure of a business, including the various relationships between the different parts of the business.
This brand has a totally credible <u>business model</u> and a promising future.

distribution channel
(distribution channels)
N-COUNT
A company's **distribution channel** is the method it uses in order to distribute its goods.
Online booking led to a radical shakeup of <u>distribution channels</u> and the role of travel agents.

marketing mix
N-UNCOUNT
A company's **marketing mix** is the combination of marketing activities that it uses in order to promote a particular product or service.
The product is the most important element of the <u>marketing mix</u>, since it holds together promotion, distribution and pricing policies.

feature
(features)
N-COUNT
A **feature** of a product is an interesting or important part or characteristic of it.
The improved version focuses on security enhancements, but the company has given few details about the product's <u>features</u>.

benefit
(benefits)
N-VAR
The **benefits** of a system or policy are the good results that come from it.
The important issue is keeping long-term <u>benefits</u> and costs in mind, as well as short-term ones.

marketing
N-UNCOUNT
COLLOCATIONS
a marketing – campaign / strategy / tool / consultant / slogan / tactic

The phrase *marketing mix* was first coined by Neil Borden in 1953 at an American Marketing Association meeting.

TASKS

Exercise 1

Match each paragraph with one of 'the four Ps' below.

price	*promotion*	*place*	*product*

1. This is more commonly known as the distribution channel. The arrival of the Internet had a huge impact on how and where companies made their products available to customers.
2. How much the goods or services cost the customer will depend on the competitive environment and customer demand.
3. This refers to what the goods or services consist of and includes:
   - *features – what it does*
   - *appearance – how it looks*
   - *packaging – how it is presented to the customer*
4. This includes advertising, PR [public relations], sales and sales promotions, for example *buy one get one free*. The Internet and social media forced companies to rethink how they promote their goods or services and to rethink their business models.

Exercise 2

Match each **feature** *to a related* **benefit**.

features:	***benefits:***
1. The music player is small and lightweight.	**a.** You can take photos any time, anywhere.
2. The information is updated in real time.	**b.** It's easy to carry it around with you, wherever you go.
3. The movie was filmed in 3D.	**c.** Your experience feels more realistic.
4. The phone has a camera.	**d.** You can stay aware of the latest developments as they happen.

Exercise 3

Read the text below, and then decide whether the statements that follow are **true** *or* **false**.

> Fizz, the company most of us recognize as an airline or music company, also owns cinemas. Through the distribution channel of its cinemas it is able to promote its own version of a cola soft drink. By controlling the channel of distribution it is able to be competitive in the cola market.

1. Fizz owns an airline, a music company and a chain of cinemas.
2. Fizz promotes its own brand of cola through its airline.
3. Fizz's cola is competitive because the company controls the channel of distribution.

Reflection

How did the Internet and social media affect marketing activities?
What do you think are the main benfits of online shopping?

TOPIC 3.2 Promotion

Promotion is about how a company tells its customers about its products and services.

See also

Topic 3.1 **marketing mix**

advertising agency
(advertising agencies)

N-COUNT

An **advertising agency** is a company whose business is to create advertisements for other companies or organizations.

The campaign was created by a British advertising agency.

word of mouth

PHRASE

If news or information passes by **word of mouth**, people tell it to each other rather than it being printed in written form.

Our reputation has begun spreading purely by word of mouth.

public relations

N-UNCOUNT

Public relations is the part of an organization's work that is concerned with obtaining the public's approval for what it does. The abbreviation **PR** is often used.

The move was good public relations.

N-PLURAL

You can refer to the opinion that the public has of an organization as **public relations**.

The company's public relations are disastrous.

public relations/PR

N-UNCOUNT

COLLOCATIONS

a public relations/PR firm / campaign / exercise / consultant / coup / offensive / stunt / disaster

advertising

N-UNCOUNT

Advertising is the activity of creating advertisements and making sure that people see them.

We offer digital marketing and Internet advertising technology and services.

site

N-COUNT

COLLOCATIONS

an Internet / a social networking / an official / to visit a / to access a / to launch a / to develop a / to block a site

viral marketing

N-UNCOUNT

Viral marketing is a way of promoting products which relies on individuals talking about adverts or sending Internet adverts to friends.

Using the Internet for viral marketing is a cheap, speedy way for marketers to get their message across.

social media

N-PLURAL

Social media are forms of Internet communication which allow users to communicate, publish material and interact with each other.

Social media offer companies a powerful channel through which to promote their wares and test new products.

billboard
(billboards)

N-COUNT

A **billboard** is a very large board on which posters are displayed.

We saw huge billboards advertising new housing developments.

website
(websites)

N-COUNT

A **website** is a set of information about a particular subject which is available on the Internet.

The website also features a comprehensive photo gallery.

A **site** is the same as a **website**.
The site earns its revenue from advertisers.

TASKS

Exercise 1

Are the following statements ***true*** *or* ***false****?*

1. Viral marketing is very slow and costly.
2. Social media can be used to promote products and services.
3. Word of mouth advertising is very expensive.
4. Advertising agencies create new product campaigns.
5. A PR campaign could help to improve a company's image.

Exercise 2

Use the terms in the box to complete the paragraph.

billboards	*campaign*	*Internet sites*	*word of mouth*
advertised	*viral marketing*	*social media*	*advertising agency*

Companies will often employ an **(a)**__________ or marketing consultancy to advise on and put together a marketing **(b)**__________. Traditionally products and services were **(c)**__________ on TV and radio in commercials, in newspaper ads, and on **(d)**__________ by the side of the road or street. But increasingly companies are advertising on **(e)**__________. One development has been **(f)**__________ where individuals pass adverts which they like on to friends. This is very much like making **(g)**__________ recommendations. Increasingly, companies communicate with their customers through the Internet or **(h)**__________ such as *Twitter* or *Facebook*. The result of this is that communication has become a two-way process with companies listening to their customers much more in the new marketplace.

Exercise 3

Put these four media types into the correct place in the table.

a. social media **b.** TV **c.** newspapers **d.** billboards

Media type	Advantages	Disadvantages
1.	very good for short sharp messages	can be affected by the weather
2.	can be targeted	may be totally ignored by recipient
3.	can provide a lot of detail/ information	a company's advertisement may be 'lost' amongst many others, possibly those of its rivals
4.	can demonstrate the product in use	consumers may not pay attention

Mini Webquest

- Find some examples of interesting viral marketing campaigns.

TOPIC 3.3 Price, packaging and place

With the arrival of the Internet, it has become much easier for customers to compare the price of the same product or service from different retailers. Similarly, they have much more choice about where they buy the product or service from. How a product is packaged often raises environmental concerns with customers.

See also	
Topic 3.1	**demand, distribution channel**

price

list price
(list prices)

N-COUNT

The **list price** of something is its official price, before any discounts are included.

The list price of the car is £20,000.

You can also call the list price the **recommended retail price**, or **rrp**.

price-sensitive
ADJ

If the market for a product or service is **price-sensitive**, it is quickly affected by changes in price.

Online shoppers are extremely price-sensitive, and they tend to compare prices on a variety of sites.

market price
(market prices)

N-COUNT

If you talk about the **market price** of something, you mean that its price or value depends on how many of the items are available and how many people want to buy them.

The fair trade company pays above the market price for its coffee.

You can also call the market price the **market value**.

packaging

recyclable
ADJ

Recyclable waste or materials can be processed and used again.

People are asking for recyclable, biodegradable containers.

packaging
N-UNCOUNT

Packaging is the container or covering that something is sold in.

It is selling very well, in part because the packaging is so attractive.

place

online
ADJ

An **online** company or service offers customers the opportunity to order goods or use services via the Internet.

The company is now the leading online music retailer.

online
ADV

COLLOCATIONS

to buy / to purchase / to order / to book / to sell / to track / to view / to research / to browse — *something* **online**

wholesaler
(wholesalers)

N-COUNT

A **wholesaler** is a person whose business is buying large quantities of goods and selling them in smaller amounts, for example to shops.

They are the largest drugs wholesaler in Europe.

intermediary
(intermediaries)

N-COUNT

An **intermediary** is a person or organization that provides a link between two other people or organizations.

The intermediary offers services like shipping, warehousing and freight forwarding.

TASKS

Exercise 1

Online retailer new-pc.com has just received an order for a new computer from Bell Ltd. Match the terms in the box to show the process from the retailer receiving the order to the customer receiving the new computer.

local parcel delivery courier	*Bell Ltd*	*overseas shipping company*
new-pc.com	*overseas factory*	

online retailer **a.** ____________________

wholesaler **b.** ____________________

intermediary #1 **c.** ____________________

intermediary #2 **d.** ____________________

customer **e.** ____________________

Exercise 2

Use the terms in the box to complete the paragraph.

list prices	*online*	*wholesaler*	*packaging*
Internet	*recyclable*	*intermediary*	

(a)____________________ not only promotes or helps sell a product, but it also gives information about the product, stores and transports the product. These days customers look for and many governments require packaging that is **(b)**____________________ and not wasteful. Most producers sell through an **(c)**____________________ or third party, such as a **(d)**____________________ who then sells to the retailer. Consumer products are more and more sold over the **(e)**____________________ on outlet websites such as *Amazon*, which started as an **(f)**____________________ book retailer but now sells a huge range of consumer products. Most online retailers offer discounts on the official **(g)**____________________.

Exercise 3

Look at the following prices for the same product, shown on a price comparison website, and answer the questions below.

RETAILER	CUSTOMER RATING	PRICE	DELIVERY
Zedex	**	$100 *(list price $140)*	21-35 days
Sanderson	***	$120 *(list price $140)*	1-2 days
Tri-Lite	*****	$129 *(list price $140)*	7 days

1. Which online retailer is offering the best reduction on the list price?
2. Who is selling closest to the list price?
3. Which company can deliver the fastest?
4. Who has the best customer rating?
5. Who has the worst customer rating?

Mini Webquest

- Use a price comparison website to find the best price for a product that you would like to buy.

TOPIC 3.4 Branding

Branding refers to the image or impression that a company creates for its products, usually through promotion.

See also	
Topic 3.5	**diversification**

brand

(brands)

N-COUNT

A **brand** of a product is the version of it that is made by one particular manufacturer.

Consumers were less willing to purchase items from a smaller online retailer than a large well-known brand.

own brand

(own brands)

N-COUNT

Own brands are products which have the trademark or label of the shop which sells them, especially a supermarket chain. They are normally cheaper than other popular brands.

Buy supermarket own brands wherever possible.

An own brand can also be called an **own label**.

brand name

(brand names)

N-COUNT

The **brand name** of a product is the name that the manufacturer gives it and under which it is sold.

These manufacturers have strong brand names and well-established global operations.

brand

N-COUNT

COLLOCATIONS

to market / to build / to launch / to promote / to advertise / to establish / to trust — a brand

brand awareness

N-UNCOUNT

Brand awareness is how much people know about a particular brand, and the opinions and ideas that they have about it.

We want to raise brand awareness in this country.

brand image

(brand images)

N-COUNT

The **brand image** of a particular brand is the image or impression that people have of it, usually created by advertising.

The company believes it can continue to generate customers due to its strong brand image.

brand loyalty

N-UNCOUNT

Brand loyalty is the way some people always buy a particular brand of product, and are not likely to start buying a different brand.

Part of their success has been in their ability to deliver products attractive to young people, building brand loyalty.

brand stretch

N-UNCOUNT

Brand stretch is when a company uses an existing brand name to sell a new product. They do this because they think that people who buy the existing products with that brand name will also buy the new ones.

They want to pursue a strategy of brand extension, or brand stretch, from clothing into chairs and sofas.

You can also call brand stretch **brand extension**.

brand recognition

N-UNCOUNT

Brand recognition is when a person knows what a product is or knows something about it as soon as they see it or hear its name.

The online music service has major brand recognition.

TASKS

Exercise 1

Use the terms in the box to complete the paragraph.

brand awareness	*brand image*	*own brand*	*brand name*

A brand of a product is a version of it made by one particular manufacturer. Consumers may or may not recognize a particular **(a)** ________________ . This knowledge, or lack of it, is measured in terms of brand recognition and **(b)**________________ . A product sold by a retailer under the retailer's own name rather than the manufacturer's, is an **(c)**________________ product. Part of the process of making a product different from other similar ones requires a company to develop a strong **(d)**________________ for the products in its product mix.

Exercise 2

Look at the seven word partners with the word 'brand', then match each one to one of the comments below.

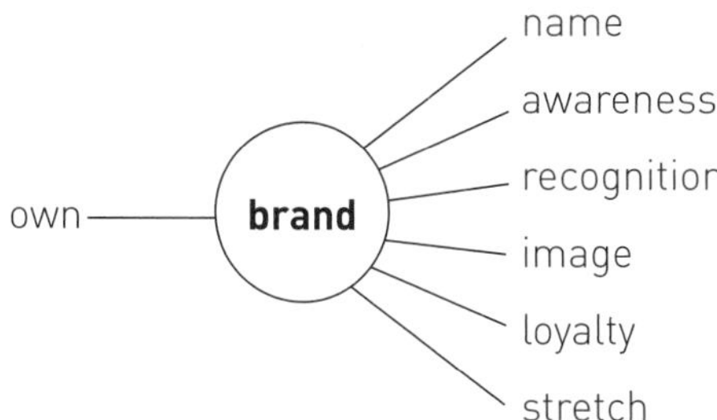

1. When ice-cream bars were first launched, I could pick out the Jupiter ice-cream bar straight away because the packaging was so familiar.
2. I always buy Worthit shampoo because it's just as good as a branded product, but much cheaper.
3. I always buy their jeans. I would never buy any other brand.
4.  Cool-Cola is the most famous one I can think of.
5. I love the adverts. I think they've made the drink seem really appealing.
6. I don't know anything about the different mobile phones on the market, I'm afraid.
7. I think companies that use a famous name on lots of products just make the brand seem cheap.

Exercise 3

*Are these statements **true** or **false**?*

	True	**False**
1. Own label products sell at higher prices than branded products.	☐	☐
2. The purpose of developing a brand image is to enable consumers to identify with a product.	☐	☐
3. Memorable brand names are often long and complicated.	☐	☐
4. The diversification of a brand name can be a failure if it weakens the brand's core values.	☐	☐

Reflection

Is it important to you whether you buy brand name or own brand products?
Have you ever worked for a company with a strong brand image?

TOPIC 3.5 Marketing strategies

Companies can adopt different marketing strategies to suit the products or services that they are launching. They may need to change their strategy to reflect recent changes in the marketplace, for example the emergence of a new competitor.

See also			
Topic 3.1	**marketing mix**	Topic 10.5	**dilute**
Topic 3.4	**brand**		

penetration pricing

N-UNCOUNT

Penetration pricing is the policy of setting a relatively low price for goods or services in order to encourage sales.

Undercutting competitors is known as penetration pricing, where a company sets a low price to increase sales and market share.

USP

(USPs)

N-COUNT

The **USP** of a product or service is a particular feature of it which can be used in advertising to show how it is different from, and better than, other similar products or services. **USP** is an abbreviation for 'Unique Selling Point'.

With Volvo, safety was always the USP.

competition-based pricing

N-UNCOUNT

Competition-based pricing is the policy of setting a price for goods or services based on the price charged by other companies for similar goods or services.

We use competition-based pricing to maximize market share.

pricing strategy

(pricing strategies)

N-COUNT

A company's **pricing strategy** is the system of prices that it sets for the goods it produces or the service it provides.

The airline has extended its low-fare pricing strategy for short domestic routes to longer routes essential to business.

cost-based pricing

N-UNCOUNT

Cost-based pricing is the policy of setting a price for goods or services based on how much it costs to produce, distribute and market them.

Unlike cost-based pricing, in value-based pricing, a company sets its target-price based on the customer's value perceptions.

value-based pricing

N-UNCOUNT

Value-based pricing is the policy of setting a price for goods or services based on the customer's perception of value.

The company should move to a more value-based pricing model in line with overall profit improvement rather than unit cost.

strategy

N-COUNT

COLLOCATIONS

a marketing / a pricing / an investment / a growth / an expansion / a business — strategy

SWOT

N-UNCOUNT

SWOT is a system that companies use to examine how well they are working, in order to help them improve and make plans for the future. **SWOT** is an abbreviation for 'strengths, weaknesses, opportunities and threats'.

A SWOT analysis provides a good structuring device for sorting out ideas about the future and a company's ability to exploit that future.

diversification

N-UNCOUNT

Diversification is when a company starts to produce new and different goods or services.

Our aim is to improve long-term profitability through a sustainable program of geographical expansion and diversification.

Brand managers are often concerned that diversification can lead to *brand dilution* and confusion on the part of customers about what the brand represents.

TASKS

Exercise 1

*Are these statements **true** or **false**?*

	True	False
1. A SWOT analysis can help a business to recognise its strengths and weaknesses.	☐	☐
2. Penetration pricing can help a company to increase its market share.	☐	☐
3. Diversification is when a company specialises in one product only.	☐	☐
4. Value-based pricing is based on how much it costs to produce a product.	☐	☐
5. A product's USP is what makes it different from, and better than, other similar products.	☐	☐

Exercise 2

Match a pricing strategy on the left with a reason the right.

1. Company 1 is using penetration pricing		**a.** to maximize value for customers and become more profitable.
2. Company 2 is using competition-based pricing		**b.** to get its products into a new market.
3. Company 3 uses cost-based pricing		**c.** because adding a percentage profit margin to the production costs is a quick and easy way of setting a price.
4. Company 4 uses value-based pricing		**d.** so that consumers won't think that their products are more expensive than those of their competitors.

Exercise 3

Read the information about the four companies and select the pricing strategy that they are most likely to use when setting the price of their product.

cost-based pricing	*penetration pricing*	*competition-based pricing*	*value-based pricing*

1. Qualfast are a new company and are very concerned to establish a large customer base. They hope to get their products into the market rapidly so that consumers will become familiar with their name.
2. Hall & Co. spend a lot of money each year carrying out market research to make sure that they know how their customers measure value.
3. Anderton Ltd. are one of many companies offering a similar service. They are concerned not to set their prices any higher than those of their main rivals.
4. Carlo Inc. is a small company with small profit margins. They are very aware of how much they spend on production, distribution and marketing.

Exercise 4

Look at the table below, which shows a SWOT matrix for a small company. Put each of the following points into the correct part of the table.

1. Diversification would increase sales in new markets
2. Loyal customer base
3. Larger competitors may take bigger market share
4. Lack of new products

Strengths	Weaknesses
Opportunities	**Threats**

Mini Webquest

- Find some examples of SWOT analysis.
- Find out about **brand dilution**.

TOPIC 4.1

What makes a good salesperson?

The key to being a good salesperson is closing the sale, but a lot of other things need to go on before that can happen.

empathize
(empathizes, empathizing, empathized)

VERB

If you **empathize** with someone, you understand their situation, problems and feelings, because you have been in a similar situation.

You should clearly empathize with a client who has concerns.

close
(closes, closing, closed)

VERB

To **close** a business deal or a sale means to complete it successfully.

We believe that the relationship with the customer does not end at closing the sale, but extends far beyond that.

persuade
(persuades, persuading, persuaded)

VERB

If you **persuade** someone to do something, you cause them to do it by giving them good reasons for doing it.

They are now trying to persuade existing customers to sign up for the new service.

read
(reads, reading, read)

VERB

If you can **read** someone or you can **read** their gestures, you can understand what they are thinking or feeling by the way that they behave or the things that they say.

If you have to work in a team you must learn to read people.

salesperson
(salespeople)

N-COUNT

A **salesperson** is a person whose job is to sell things, especially directly to shops or other businesses on behalf of a company.

She has been top salesperson at every firm she has worked for.

You can also use **salesman** for a man, or **saleswoman** for a woman.

good listener
(good listeners)

N-COUNT

If you describe someone as a **good listener**, you mean that they listen carefully and sympathetically to you when you talk, for example about your problems.

I am a very good listener; it's part of my job.

knowledgeable

ADJ

Someone who is **knowledgeable** has or shows a clear understanding of many different facts about their job or about a particular subject.

We employ friendly and knowledgeable staff.

salesperson

N-COUNT

COLLOCATIONS

a top / a professional / a successful / an excellent / an effective / an experienced — salesperson

enthusiastic

ADJ

If you are **enthusiastic** about something, you show how much you like or enjoy it by the way that you behave and talk.

Try to motivate people to become as enthusiastic about your product or service as you are.

TASKS

Exercise 1

Use the terms in the box to complete the paragraph.

close	*enthusiastic*	*salesperson*	*good listener*	*knowledgeable*	*persuade*	*reading*

A good salesperson needs to be a **(a)**____________________, and to be good at **(b)**____________________ people. This will help them to establish the customer's needs and wants, and help them to build a relationship with the customer. A good **(c)**____________________ should also be **(d)**____________________ about the product or service that they are selling, so that they can present the features and benefits effectively. If a salesperson talks about their product or service in an **(e)**____________________ manner, this will motivate customers to feel the same way, and may help to **(f)**____________________ them to buy it. This will ultimately make it easier for the salesperson to **(g)**____________________ the sale.

Exercise 2

Which of these is a good salesperson (Y) and which is not (N)?

		Y	N
1.	When I'm speaking to customers on the phone, I'm always very enthusiastic about the service that we offer.	☐	☐
2.	If customers ask me about the product that I sell, I just tell them that I've never used it.	☐	☐
3.	I'm really good at reading people, so I can tell what customers want straight away.	☐	☐
4.	Because I love the service that I'm selling, it makes it easy for me to persuade others to buy it.	☐	☐
5.	I find it difficult to empathize with customers – they're all the same to me.	☐	☐

Exercise 3

Mike works as a salesperson in a mobile phone shop in London. Read Mike's story below, then decide whether the statements that follow are true or false.

> I started working as a salesperson in a mobile phone shop last year. In the beginning, I was very enthusiastic and knowledgeable about the products. But I often found it difficult to close sales with customers, and I couldn't understand why. Last month I went on a sales course. This taught me to identify the customers' needs and wants to help find the best product for them and make the sale. Now I'm a much better listener, which has helped me to persuade more customers of the benefits of the phones, and I've managed to close more sales this month.

1. Mike did not know much about mobile phones when he started his job.

2. Mike was enthusiastic when he started his job.

3. Mike found it easy to close sales with customers when he started his job.

4. The sales course taught Mike to find out what customers need and want.

5. After the sales course, Mike became a better listener.

6. After the sales course, Mike found it easier to persuade customers to buy phones.

7. This month, Mike didn't close any sales.

Reflection

Do you think you would make a good salesperson? Why/why not?
What qualities do you think are most important in a salesperson?

TOPIC 4.2 Orders and stock control

Availability of goods or services is a key objective for businesses. If it isn't there, the customer can't buy it.

on order

PHRASE

Something that is **on order** at a shop or factory has been asked for but has not yet been supplied.

We've despatched all we have – the rest are on order from the supplier.

stock

(stocks, stocking, stocked)

VERB

If a shop **stocks** particular goods, it keeps a supply of them to sell.

We regularly stock organic cheeses.

N-UNCOUNT

A shop's **stock** is the total amount of goods that it has available to sell.

We don't seem to have any in stock at the moment.

N-VAR

A company's **stock** is the raw materials or components that it has ready to be made into finished goods.

The buyer ordered £20,000 worth of stock.

order

(orders, ordering, ordered)

N-COUNT

An **order** is a request for something to be brought, made or obtained for you in return for money.

To reduce costs the firm should place large orders at infrequent intervals.

VERB

When you **order** something that you are going to pay for, you ask for it to be brought to you, sent to you or obtained for you.

Customers can order groceries online, then have them delivered to their homes.

logistics

N-UNCOUNT

Logistics is the management of the flow of materials through an organization, from raw materials to the finished product and also the management of distribution.

We need an efficient transport and logistics chain to carry Australian goods to international markets.

re-order level

(re-order levels)

N-COUNT

The **re-order level** of a particular stock is the point at which the existing stock becomes so low that new stock needs to be ordered.

The re-order level will depend upon the rate of usage of the stock.

stock control

N-UNCOUNT

Stock control is the activity of making sure that a company has the right amount of goods available to sell.

With better demand planning we can cut a lot of wastage and improve stock control.

purchasing department

(purchasing departments)

N-COUNT

The **purchasing department** of a company is the section that is responsible for buying products, components or materials.

Company purchasing departments are looking for greater visibility of what IT budgets are spent on.

lead time

(lead times)

N-COUNT

The **lead time**, in this context, is the period of time that it takes for goods to be delivered after someone has ordered them.

Order lead time is the period from the moment the customer first places the order or request (including repairs) until it is received.

TASKS

Exercise 1

Use the terms in the box to complete the paragraph.

stocks	*lead times*	*orders*	*components*

Most manufacturing companies have a warehouse full of **(a)**________________ waiting to be assembled. These parts are known as stocks. Keeping **(b)**________________ low reduces the need to finance, store and handle them. In order to do this, manufacturers get their suppliers to make and deliver components just before they are needed. This shortens **(c)**________________, or the time that it takes to make and deliver goods, or to fill customers' **(d)**________________.

Exercise 2

Whitewash, a washing machine manufacturer, has several suppliers of the raw materials and components that it needs to produce its machines. Read the text and answer the questions.

> Businesses purchase raw materials, semi-finished goods and components, which they use to produce products that they can sell to consumers and other businesses. The purchasing department of a firm deals with suppliers and maintains adequate stock levels. Managing the materials is an important part of any business. Logistics is the term used to describe the management of the flow of materials through an organization, from raw materials to finished goods.

1. What is the term used to describe the management of materials through a company?
2. Who is responsible for maintaining the stock levels that Whitewash needs to produce the finished washing machines?
3. Whitewash buys metal, electric motors and other parts needed to assemble its machines. Which is an example of a raw material, and which is an example of a component?
4. Whitewash sells 70% of their finished products through their chain of retail outlets. The other 30% are sold to other businesses. Which of the following businesses do you think are customers of Whitewash?
   manufacturers of consumer goods, hotels, launderettes, firms of architects

Exercise 3

*Are the sentences **true** or **false**?*

1. If you have a product on order you are waiting for it to be delivered.
2. Re-order levels do not depend on the level of stock.
3. The term 'stocks' can cover supplies of raw materials, components and finished products.
4. Customers are usually happier with short lead times than with long lead times.

Mini Webquest

- Find out about the main logistics companies in your country.
- What is the range of services that they offer?

TOPIC 4.3

Distribution

The distribution of goods involves supplying or delivering them to a number of people or places. A distributor is a company that supplies goods to shops or other businesses.

See also	
Topic 3.1	**distribution channel**

distribution network

(distribution networks)

N-COUNT

A **distribution network** is a set of distribution chains.

Our strengthened worldwide distribution network puts us in an excellent position to continue our global growth.

warehousing

N-UNCOUNT

Warehousing is the act of storing materials or goods in a warehouse.

The major costs incurred by wholesalers are transport and warehousing costs.

warehouse

(warehouses)

N-COUNT

A **warehouse** is a large building where raw materials or manufactured goods are stored until they are exported to other countries or distributed to shops to be sold.

They are Canada's largest operator of cold-storage warehouses.

distribution chain

(distribution chains)

N-COUNT

A **distribution chain** is all the stages that goods pass through between leaving a factory and arriving at a retailer.

We've electronically linked every step of the distribution chain from manufacturing to sale and delivery.

A distribution chain can also be called a **supply chain**.

distribution

N-UNCOUNT

COLLOCATIONS

distribution
- channel
- system
- centre
- hub
- warehouse
- methods
- of *something*

freight

N-UNCOUNT

Freight is the movement of goods by lorries, trains, ships or aeroplanes.

We believe that air freight should only be used when road, rail and sea options have been fully considered and discounted.

N-UNCOUNT

Freight is also the goods that are transported by lorries, trains, ships or aeroplanes.

Our ships carry freight between Asia, Europe and North America.

forwarding

N-UNCOUNT

Forwarding is the collection, transportation and delivery of goods.

She is an export assistant for a forwarding firm in Melbourne.

Forwarding can also be called **freight forwarding**.

end user

(end users)

N-COUNT

The **end user** of a product or service is the user that it has been designed for, rather than the person who installs or maintains it, or indeed who bought it.

The application enables end-users to manage groups of contact-centre agents more easily.

agent

(agents)

N-COUNT

An **agent** is a person who looks after someone else's business affairs or does business on their behalf.

You are buying direct, rather than through an agent.

TASKS

Exercise 1

Use the terms in the box to complete the paragraph.

distribution network	*end users*	*distribution*
warehouse	*distributor*	*agent*

(a)________________ is concerned with getting a product to the customers (or, for technical products, **(b)**________________). The **(c)**________________ makes the product available to the customers through various retail outlets. Products may be distributed directly to retailers, or through a **(d)**________________ to wholesalers, who store the goods in a **(e)**________________. The wholesalers then forward the products to the retailers or retail outlets. Some businesses use an **(f)**________________ to bring buyers and sellers together, who works on a commission basis.

Exercise 2

Label the diagram using the terms in the box.

manufacturers	*wholesaler*	*end users*	*agent*	*warehouse*

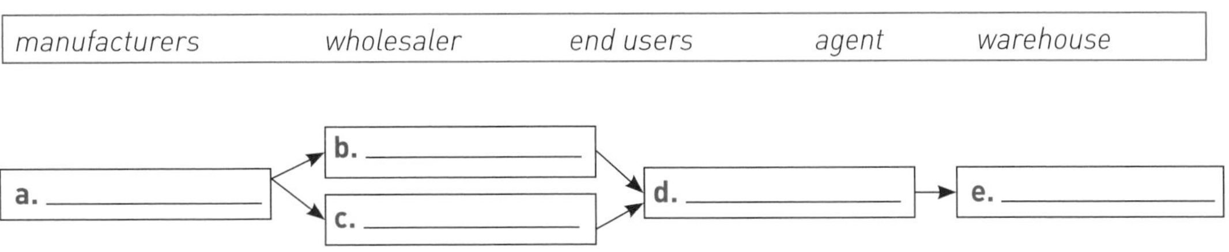

Exercise 3

Read this dictionary entry (from the Collins Dictionary of Economics) and answer the questions.

Freight forwarder or forwarding agent a firm that specializes in the physical movement of goods in transit, arranging the collection of goods from factories, depots, etc., and delivering them direct to the customer in the case of domestic consignments and to sea-ports, airports, etc. in the case of exported goods. In the latter case, the forwarder also handles the booking arrangements and the documentation required by the customs authorities.

1. Find three terms that refer to a firm specializing in the movement of goods.
2. Which word is used in the text to mean freight?
3. In a domestic context the forwarding agent offers a delivery service to the customer from which two places?
4. Where does the freight forwarding company take goods for export?

Mini Webquest

- Find out about the **hub and spoke** system of distribution.

TOPIC 4.4 Sales methods

Methods of selling have been transformed by the Internet, for both B2B and B2C.

sales methods

B2C

N-UNCOUNT

B2C is the selling of goods and services by businesses to consumers, especially using the Internet. **B2C** is an abbreviation for 'business to consumer'.

The e-commerce boom saw an estimated 77 % growth in B2C transactions.

B2B

N-UNCOUNT

B2B is the selling of goods and services by one company to another, especially using the Internet. **B2B** is an abbreviation for 'business to business'.

We'll help you find suppliers and buyers both domestically and globally in the B2B marketplace.

online retail

N-UNCOUNT

Online retail is the business or activity of selling goods or services via the Internet.

I own a small online retail company.

online shopping

N-UNCOUNT

Online shopping is the activity of buying goods and services via the Internet.

Limited product offerings and poor customer service in the high street are increasing online shopping.

home shopping

N-UNCOUNT

Home shopping is the activity of buying things from an online retailer or from a TV shopping channel.

The home shopping fashion retailer reported their profits were up by 18 per cent.

cold call

(cold calls, cold calling, cold called)

N-COUNT

If someone makes a **cold call**, they telephone or visit someone they have never contacted, without making an appointment, in order to try and sell them something.

The way to deal with cold calls is with politeness and good humour.

VERB

To **cold call** means to make a cold call.

She started cold calling and visiting stores offering samples.

direct mail

N-UNCOUNT

Direct mail is a method of marketing which involves companies sending advertising material directly to people who they think may be interested in their products.

The biggest users of direct mail remain financial services, catalogue companies and charities.

People who receive direct mail often refer to it as **junk mail** because they have not asked for it and do not want it.

sample

(samples)

N-COUNT

A **sample** of a substance or product is a small quantity of it that shows you what it is like.

Providing free samples is a major marketing necessity for our industry.

TASKS

Exercise 1

Read the text answer the questions.

Selling goods or services via the Internet is known as online retail. Online retail is an increasingly popular method of distribution. It suits both the customers, who can choose how and when to shop, and companies, who do not have to hand over part of their profits to intermediaries. The travel industry, for example, was transformed by the introduction of online booking. Online shopping is popular because consumers can buy products or services from their own home.

1. What is online retail?
2. Why do companies like online retail?
3. Name an industry that was transformed by online booking.
4. Why do customers like to shop online?

Exercise 2

Match each of the sales methods in the box to one of the comments.

free samples	*online retail*	*cold calls*	*direct mail*

1. I really hate it when someone phones me at home and starts trying to sell me something.
2. It's OK for buying books or downloading music files, because seeing them on the screen is all you need.
3. Yesterday some people were handing out sachets of shampoo at the railway station. I used it today and it's really good, so I think I'll buy some.
4. I get so much junk mail through the post – I put most of it straight in the bin.

Exercise 3

Which of the following are examples of B2B transactions and which are examples of B2C transactions?

1. an online music store selling music downloads to a customer
2. a software developer selling to large organizations
3. a clothing company using social media to sell to customers
4. a manufacturer supplying components to an electronics company
5. a person buying shoes from a high street store
6. a person using online banking

Reflection

What do you think are the best methods for a business to connect with consumers? What kinds of products or services have you shopped for online recently?

TOPIC 4.5 Retailing

Retailing is the act of selling to the public, usually in small quantities, and can include delivery and after-sales care.

retailer

(retailers)

N-COUNT

A **retailer** is a person or business that sells goods direct to the public.

The online retailer offers new Internet customers a facility to create a 'favourites' shopping list.

retail outlet

(retail outlets)

N-COUNT

A **retail outlet** is a shop or other place that sells goods direct to the public.

All sorts of retail outlets, from supermarkets to corner shops, now have what is known in the trade as 'Food For Now' zones.

merchandising

N-UNCOUNT

Merchandising is used to refer to the way that shops and businesses organize the sale of their products, for example the way that they are displayed and the prices that are chosen.

I work with the visual merchandising department on some window display concepts.

retail

N-UNCOUNT

COLLOCATIONS

a retail outlet / park / giant / sales

online / fashion / street-level / high-end retail

point of sale

(points of sale)

N-COUNT

The **point of sale** is the place in a shop where a product is passed from the seller to the customer. The abbreviation **POS** is also used.

Customer in-store notices have been displayed at the entrance of the stores, in the windows and at the point of sale.

loyalty card

(loyalty cards)

N-COUNT

A **loyalty card** is a plastic card that some shops give to regular customers. Each time the customer buys something from the shop, points are electronically stored on their card and can be exchanged later for goods or services.

Customers can register their loyalty card details on the retailer's web site.

checkout

(checkouts)

N-COUNT

In a supermarket, a **checkout** is a counter where you pay for things that you are buying.

The retailer claims around 25 per cent of its UK customers pay for goods via self-service checkouts.

bar code

(bar codes)

N-COUNT

A **bar code** is an arrangement of numbers and parallel lines that is printed on products to be sold in shops. The **bar code** can be read by computers.

Consumers can use their mobile phone to scan bar codes and view live data about products.

TASKS

Exercise 1

Use the terms in the box to complete the paragraph.

bar code	*merchandising*	*loyalty cards*
point of sale	*retail outlet*	*checkout*

When you pay for your goods at the supermarket **(a)**____________________ they are passed over a laser, which reads the **(b)**____________________ on the packaging. Merchandising is an attempt to influence the customer at the **(c)**____________________. This could be at a supermarket, car showroom or any other **(d)**____________________. **(e)**____________________ aims to encourage sales of a product by persuading customers to buy it based on its physical appeal, the way it is displayed, or even through the use of smells and lighting. Some retailers use **(f)**____________________ to encourage customers to shop with them again.

Exercise 2

Which of the following are features of merchandising?

1. creating an appropriate ambience
2. maintaining the stock levels in shops
3. designing the layout of the stores
4. displaying the products attractively
5. setting the price
6. collecting customer data

Exercise 3

Match each retailer to the correct product.

Retailer	Product
1. fashion retailer	**a.** a music download
2. bakery	**b.** a new car
3. bookshop	**c.** a pair of shoes
4. car showroom	**d.** a loaf of bread
5. online music store	**e.** a textbook

Reflection

What kind of things do you buy face-to-face and not online?
Why is this?

TOPIC 5.1 Customer care

Customer care or after-sales care is about looking after your customers so that they stay with your products or services, do not go looking for alternative sources of supply, and are encouraged to buy further products or services.

customer needs

N-PLURAL

Customer needs are the things that a customer requires or wants from a service or product.

Success is based on effectively meeting customer needs.

customer loyalty

N-UNCOUNT

Customer loyalty is when a person continues to buy products from the same shop or company over a long period of time.

For the supermarkets, these programs encourage customer loyalty.

repeat customer

(repeat customers)

N-COUNT

If a company gets **repeat customers**, people who have bought their goods or services before buy them again.

Over a third of the business comes from repeat customers.

customer satisfaction

N-UNCOUNT

When customers are pleased with the goods or services that they have bought, you can refer to **customer satisfaction**.

Customer satisfaction with their mobile service runs at more than 90 per cent.

customer base

(customer bases)

N-COUNT

A business's **customer base** is all its regular customers, considered as a group.

The bank has a customer base of 21 million people.

You can also call a customer base a **client base**.

customer care

N-UNCOUNT

COLLOCATIONS

to provide / to handle / to deliver / to manage **customer care**

customer service

N-UNCOUNT

The term **customer service** refers to the way that companies behave towards their customers, for example how well they treat them.

Their mail order business has a strong reputation for customer service.

customer retention

(customer retentions)

N-UNCOUNT

Customer retention is the actions that a business carries out to keep customers using their products or services.

It's vital to have a strategy for customer retention.

N-COUNT

Customer retention is the number of customers that continue to use a product or service.

We want to increase sales and improve customer retention rates.

customer experience

(customer experiences)

N-VAR

The term **customer experience** refers to all the experiences that a customer has during their relationship with a business.

Every feature of the store is dedicated to improving the customer experience.

TASKS

Exercise 1

Does the speaker in each sentence offer their client good customer care?

1. Whenever I've had an unhappy client, I've dealt with the problem face-to-face rather than by telephone or in writing.
2. If a client asks me for help that I'm not really qualified to give, I tell them what I think they want to hear.
3. One of our distributors failed to deliver goods to a very important client. Because we had employed the distributor I took full responsibility for the problem.

Exercise 2

Complete each box in the flow chart with one of these terms:

1. customer needs
2. customer satisfaction
3. repeat customers
4. customer loyalty
5. customer care

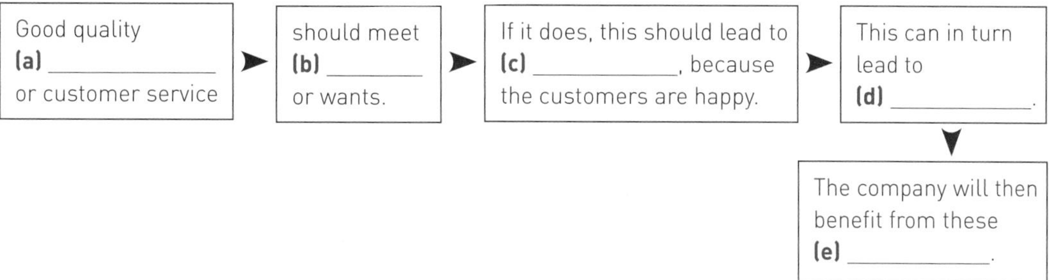

Exercise 3

Look at the chart showing customer retention levels for three telecoms companies over four years. Answer the questions which follow.

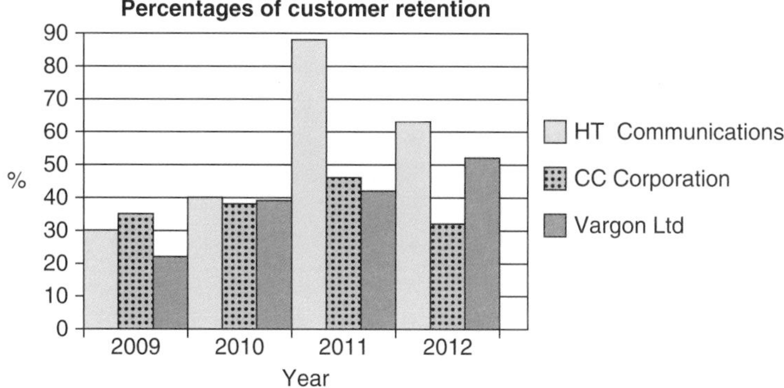

1. Which company had the lowest customer retention in 2012?
2. Which company had the highest customer retention in 2011?
3. Whose customer retention level has continued to rise every year?
4. When did HT Communications have their highest customer retention rate?

Reflection

What, in your opinion, is good customer care?
Can you think of a time when you received bad customer care?

TOPIC 5.2

Customer feedback

Customer feedback is when customers tell a business how good or bad its products or services are, and how it could improve them. Customer complaints are a negative form of feedback but feedback can also be positive of course.

complaint

(complaints)

N-VAR

A **complaint** is a statement in which a customer expresses their dissatisfaction with a particular product or service.

If the complaint is not resolved satisfactorily and you want to take it further, you'll need to make a written complaint.

refund

(refunds)

N-COUNT

A **refund** is a sum of money which is returned to you, for example because you have paid too much or because you have returned goods to a shop.

Feedback on their website is glowing, and they promise that if a customer is unhappy with their purchase they will provide a full refund.

criticize

(criticizes, criticizing, criticized)

VERB

If you **criticize** someone or something, you express your disapproval of them by saying what you think is wrong with them.

Consumer groups have criticized the government for not revealing the names of retail stores involved in food recalls.

feedback

N-UNCOUNT

COLLOCATIONS

to request / to seek / to welcome / to give / to provide / to receive / to analyse — feedback

praise

(praises, praising, praised)

VERB

If you **praise** someone or something, you express your approval for their achievements or qualities.

The company has been highly praised for its environmentally friendly policies.

patient

ADJ

If you are **patient**, you stay calm and do not get annoyed, for example when something takes a long time, or when someone is not doing what you want them to do.

The airline has urged customers to be patient, saying 'some delays may be expected'.

courteous

ADJ

Someone who is **courteous** is polite and respectful to other people.

The staff are friendly, courteous, helpful, informed and always smiling.

attentive

ADJ

If you are **attentive**, you are paying close attention to what is being said or done.

The businesses that thrive will be those that are obsessively attentive to what customers want.

TASKS

Exercise 1

Use the terms in the box to complete the paragraph.

refund	*praise*	*feedback*	*complaints*

Customer **(a)** ____________________ provides an opportunity to find out what your clients want and need from you, and so improve your level of service or the quality of your goods. Positive feedback is when customers **(b)** ____________________ your products or service. Negative feedback is when customers make **(c)** ____________________ about your products or service. If feedback is particularly negative, you may decide to offer the customer a **(d)** ____________________.

Exercise 2

Match each of the following words with one that has the same meaning.

1. patient	**a.** kind
2. courteous	**b.** calm
3. attentive	**c.** polite
4. sympathetic	**d.** alert

Exercise 3

Read the text and then say whether the following sentences are ***true*** *or* ***false****.*

Customer feedback is associated most with the service sector where service providers often ask clients to complete or fill in forms or questionnaires about their experience of the service, for example guests in a hotel. But feedback may also be received via emails, letters, phone calls or face-to-face. When you receive a customer complaint in person or on the phone, you must try to be patient, courteous and sympathetic. You also need to listen attentively to find out exactly what the problem is and record all the details. You should always apologize and promise follow-up action. Never argue or get angry with the customer.

	True	False
1. Customer feedback is not normally used within the service sector.	☐	☐
2. Filling in forms or sending an email are two ways of giving customer feedback.	☐	☐
3. You should be polite and sympathetic when you get a customer complaint.	☐	☐
4. You do not need to listen carefully to customer feedback.	☐	☐
5. You should record or write down what the problem is.	☐	☐
6. You should never apologize or make any promises.	☐	☐
7. Sometimes it's OK to get angry with customers.	☐	☐

Mini Webquest

- Find customer feedback forms online for a service or product that you enjoy.

Reflection

Have you ever made a customer complaint?
What kind of response did you receive?

TOPIC 5.3 Customer relationship management

Customer relationship management (CRM) is the strategic use of information technology (IT) to manage the way in which we talk to customers, from the moment we speak for the first time to a prospective customer, to the delivery of the order.

See also
Topic 13.3 **ERP**

prospective

ADJ

You use **prospective** to describe someone who wants to be the thing mentioned or who is likely to be the thing mentioned.

Making prospective clients aware of the firm and of the advantages of its services is essential.

analyse

(analyses, analysing, analysed)

VERB

If you **analyse** something, you consider it carefully or use statistical methods in order to fully understand it.

Deal making is the ability to analyse orders online and evaluate their attractiveness before making a commitment.

chase

(chases, chasing, chased)

VERB

If you **chase** something that is needed or needs dealing with, you find it or find out what is being done about it.

We will chase payments that have not been made.

track

(tracks, tracking, tracked)

VERB

If you **track** something, you follow its progress or development.

The system can track and trace from order to delivery.

CRM

N-UNCOUNT

COLLOCATIONS

CRM –
- software
- system
- package
- application
- installation
- vendor
- tool

CRM can require complex software tools, such as those sold by SAP, Oracle and Microsoft, to manage the workflow. In 2008 the CRM business was worth over 9 billion dollars.

log

(logs, logging, logged)

VERB

If you **log** an event or fact, you record it officially in writing or on a computer.

Every site you visit logs information about who you are and what you look at.

synchronize

(synchronizes, synchronizing, synchronized)

VERB

If you **synchronize** two activities, processes or movements, or if you **synchronize** one activity, process or movement with another, you cause them to happen at the same time and speed as each other.

Tracking begins at the loading dock when the merchandise data is scanned and synchronized with the purchase order.

flow

(flows)

N-VAR

The **flow** of information or money, or a flow of it, is the free movement of it between people or organizations.

The system links all parties in the port and shipping community, enabling real-time information flow.

TASKS

Exercise 1

Read the text and then answer the questions which follow.

Customer relationship management, or CRM, allows you and your customer to log information about prospective clients. It also allows you to record, track, analyse, manage and synchronize orders. Using CRM, you can easily exchange and share information, and you can improve information flow between you and your customer. CRM also lets you initiate payments, chase payments or make payments.

1. How does CRM help you with prospective clients?
2. What does CRM let you do with orders?
3. What does CRM allow you to share more easily?
4. What can CRM improve between you and your customer?
5. What can CRM help you do with payments?

Exercise 2

Match the two halves of the sentences.

1. Integrating CRM into a customer's business	**a.** customers and your interactions with them.
2. We are the number one CRM applications company	**b.** the service we offer our clients.
3. A CRM system tracks everything about	**c.** requires skill and experience.
4. The company will use CRM	**d.** to improve its information flow.
5. We will implement new customer relationship management (CRM) software to improve	**e.** in the world.

Exercise 3

Match each noun with the most appropriate verb below.

1. information	**a.** chase
2. orders	**b.** share
3. payments	**c.** track

Mini Webquest

- Find out about what CRM software is available to you.

TOPIC 5.4 Customer reviews

With the arrival of the Internet and social media, it is much easier for potential customers to see, in customer reviews, what actual customers think of goods or a service that they have bought.

social media

N-PLURAL

Social media are forms of Internet communication which allow users to communicate, publish material and interact with each other.

Social media tools have changed the way advertisers engage with consumers - and how consumers engage with brands.

review

(reviews)

N-COUNT

A **review** is a report that someone publishes on a website, in which they express their opinion of something, for example a product or a hotel.

Customers can quickly compare prices, reviews and customer feedback at the click of a button.

potential

ADJ

You use **potential** to say that someone or something is capable of developing into the particular kind of person or thing mentioned.

They can connect with millions of potential customers using mobile technology.

review

N-COUNT

COLLOCATIONS

an online / a helpful / a positive / a negative / a glowing / a detailed / an in-depth / a mixed — **review**

subjective

ADJ

Something that is **subjective** is based on personal opinions and feelings rather than on facts.

Most user reviews are very subjective, unlike the objective reviews from professionals.

recommend

(recommends, recommending, recommended)

VERB

If someone **recommends** a product, organization or service to you, they suggest that you would find that product, organization or service good or useful.

I have just spent a holiday there and would recommend it to anyone.

monitor

(monitors, monitoring, monitored)

VERB

If you **monitor** something, you regularly check its development or progress, and sometimes comment on it.

The website monitors your taste in music and recommends new artists.

rate

(rates, rating, rated)

VERB

If you **rate** someone or something as good or bad, you consider them to be good or bad. You can also say that someone or something rates as good or bad.

ASB was consistently rated the number one bank for customer service.

TASKS

Exercise 1

Use the terms in the box to complete the paragraph.

recommend	*subjective*	*monitor*
negative	*social media*	*reviews*

It is easy to find **(a)**____________________ of most products or services on the Internet or via **(b)**____________________. But one problem with reviews is that they contain **(c)**____________________ opinions and are often unmoderated. As a result, they can be unfairly **(d)**____________________ about the product or service that they are commenting on. They may or may not **(e)**____________________ the product or service. Producers or service providers need to **(f)**____________________ these websites to find out what people think of their products and those of their competitors.

Exercise 2

Look at this rating system and the customer reviews which follow. Which of these reviews is positive (P), negative (N) or average (A)?

rating:

* *terrible* ** *poor* *** *average* **** *very good* ***** *excellent*

1. The hotel was beautiful – I'd definitely go back! ****
2. The camera broke after 3 days – I wouldn't recommend it. *
3. I absolutely love this tune – download it now!!! *****
4. Didn't think this film was great, but it was OK. ***
5. The phone came without instructions and I still can't use it! **

Exercise 3

Match the two halves of the sentences.

1. There are millions of potential	**a.** someone's subjective opinion.
2. This criticism is just	**b.** and the results are published regularly.
3. We monitor the service very strictly,	**c.** customers in this new market.

Reflection

How much do you rely on customer reviews when choosing a product or service?

Mini Webquest

- Find out about what people have said on the Internet about a hotel you know. Do you agree with their opinions?

TOPIC 5.5 Consumer protection

Consumer protection is about the protection by law of people's rights when they buy something.

Trade Descriptions Act

N-SING

In Britain, the **Trade Descriptions Act** is a law designed to prevent companies from presenting their goods or services in a dishonest or misleading way.

This section of the Trade Descriptions Act makes it an offence to mark things in such a way that they hide the real price.

The Trade Descriptions Act can also be called the **Trades Descriptions Act**.

legislation

N-UNCOUNT

Legislation consists of a law or laws passed by a government.

Another piece of important legislation introduced minimum wages, particularly in sectors where workers were most vulnerable.

laissez-faire

N-UNCOUNT

Laissez-faire is the policy which is based on the idea that governments and the law should not interfere with business, finance or the conditions of people's working lives.

The financial crisis is an excuse to question the wisdom of laissez-faire and to advocate a bigger role for the state.

Laissez-faire governments prefer **self-regulation** to **legislation**, for example in areas of food and drink, and commodities, where the producers **police** their own industry sector.

police

(polices, policing, policed)

VERB

If a person or group in authority **polices** a law or an area of public life, they make sure that what is done is fair and legal.

Imro is a self-regulatory body that polices the investment management business.

consumer rights

N-PLURAL

Consumer rights are the legal rights that people have when they buy something.

A UK consumer rights watchdog has urged new laws to protect consumers' digital rights.

self-regulation

N-UNCOUNT

Self-regulation is the controlling of a process or activity by the people or organizations that are involved in it rather than by an outside organization such as the government.

Competition between companies is too fierce for self-regulation to work.

customer data

N-UNCOUNT

Customer data is information about a company's customers, especially information about their shopping habits, that is stored in a database.

The security of customer data is the most important part of our business.

Companies must not release this information to third parties without the permission of the customer.

Internet security

N-UNCOUNT

Internet security is the use of measures to improve the security of a website, especially in order to safeguard personal and financial information.

The study shows 30 per cent of consumers agree that Internet security threats prevent them from making more online transactions.

Data Protection Act

N-SING

In Britain, the **Data Protection Act** is a law designed to protect people against the misuse of information about them stored on computer.

Using names from a computer without permission breaches the Data Protection Act.

TASKS

Exercise 1

Use the terms in the box to complete the paragraph.

data	*rights*	*protection*

In recent years there has been a lot of interest in consumer **(a)**____________________. Competitive markets may lead firms to take advantage of consumers, by reducing the quality of the goods they offer, for example. Laws have been passed to protect consumer **(b)**____________________ in relation to safety of goods, buying on credit, food labelling and much more. In the digital age, it is also important to have laws to protect consumer **(c)**____________________, which is information about a company's customers stored in a database.

Exercise 2

Match the newspaper headlines on the left with the extracts from the story on the right.

1. Government promises new powerful data protection act	**a.** ...people's credit card details have been misused and their personal details have been passed on to other businesses without their authorisation...
2. Judges reject new consumer protection legislation	**b.** ...here, rights are especially strong on door-to-door selling and Internet security...
3. Huge questions raised over Internet security	**c.** ...in the absence of meaningful consumer rights, the rule for anyone buying anything is still 'buyer beware'...
4. Megastores prosecuted under Trade Descriptions Act	**d.** ...all citizens will have the right to see all information held by most government departments...
5. 'Consumer protection' the strongest in Europe says Government minister	**e.** ...labelling was incorrect on 32 items, and weights were wrong on 17 out of 20 fresh items purchased by inspectors...

Exercise 3

*Are the following **true** or **false**?*

	True	False
a. Consumer laws are designed to protect businesses from dissatisfied customers.	☐	☐
b. Customer data is the information that consumers need to decide what to buy.	☐	☐
c. The Data Protection Act prohibits companies from misusing data about their customers.	☐	☐
d. The Trades Descriptions Act protects consumers.	☐	☐
e. Laissez-faire governments prefer self-regulation to legislation.	☐	☐
f. Self-regulation means that producers police their own industry sector.	☐	☐

Mini Webquest

- Find out what the equivalents are in your country or in the USA to the Trades Description and Data Protection Acts.

Module 2 People in business

For many companies, their people are their main asset. How they recruit, train, develop and manage them can be key to the ongoing success of the company.

Topic 6 Employees

6.1 Human resource management
6.2 Recruitment
6.3 Leaving a company
6.4 Remuneration
6.5 Industrial relations
6.6 Equal opportunities

Topic 7 Managers

7.1 Management
7.2 Management styles
7.3 Management roles
7.4 Change management

Topic 8 Careers, qualifications and training

8.1 Career paths
8.2 Business qualifications
8.3 Professional development and performance appraisal
8.4 Learning organizations, mentoring and coaching
8.5 Leave

TOPIC 6.1 Human resource management

Human resource management (HRM) is the work within a company that involves the recruitment, training and welfare of staff.

employee
(employees)

N-COUNT

An **employee** is a person who is paid to work for an organization or for another person.

The company recruits some 2,000 employees every month.

human resource planning

N-UNCOUNT

Human resource planning is the work within a company that involves identifying the future employment needs of the company and recruiting the staff to meet those needs.

There is a big difference between human resource planning and manpower planning.

workforce
(workforces)

N-COUNT

The **workforce** is the total number of people who are employed by a particular company.

The company employs the largest workforce in the country - 30,000 workers.

staff
(staffs)

N-COUNT-COLL

The **staff** of an organization are the people who work for it.

He had a staff of six salespeople working for him.

The staff were well informed about the products.

N-PLURAL

People who are part of a particular staff are often referred to as **staff**.

10 staff were allocated to the task.

human resources

N-UNCOUNT

Human Resources is the department in a company or organization that deals with employees, keeps their records and helps with any problems that they might have. The abbreviation **HR** is also used.

Let me introduce myself. I'm Kate from Human Resources.

You can also use **Human Resources department**.

N-PLURAL

An organization's **human resources** are the people who work for it.

Our human resources are our most important investment.

personnel

N-PLURAL

The **personnel** of an organization are the people who work for it.

The company aims to attract and retain quality personnel.

N-UNCOUNT

Personnel is the department in a large company or organization that deals with employees, keeps their records and helps with any problems that they might have.

Her first job was in Personnel.

You can also use **Personnel department**.

self-employed

ADJ

If you are **self-employed**, you organize your own work and taxes and are paid by people for a service that you provide, rather than being paid a regular salary by a person or a firm.

There are no paid holidays or sick leave if you are self-employed.

freelance

ADJ

Someone who does **freelance** work or who is, for example, a **freelance** journalist or photographer, is not employed by one organization, but is paid for each piece of work that they do by the organization that they do it for.

She is a freelance journalist.

ADV

If you work **freelance**, you do freelance work.

He is now working freelance from his home in Hampshire.

TASKS

Exercise 1

Use the terms in the box to complete the sentences.

freelance	*employee*	*self-employed*
planning	*staff*	*human resources*

The **(a)**__________________ department is responsible for recruiting and looking after the **(b)**__________________ in a company. When a new **(c)**__________________ joins the company, they usually have to fill in records for HR. In addition to employees, human resource **(d)**__________________ may involve sub-contracting work or specific tasks to **(e)**__________________ individuals or to small specialist companies. For example, a company may plan to sub-contract work to a freelance web designer or a **(f)**__________________ translator.

Exercise 2

Put each of the words under the correct heading.

a. employee **b.** staff **c.** worker **d.** workforce **e.** freelancer

Individual term	Collective term

Exercise 3

Match each term to the correct definition.

1. human resources	**a.** Deciding how to use a company's human resources most effectively.
2. human resource planning	**b.** The people employed in an organization, also known as personnel.
3. human resource management	**c.** Deciding how many, and what type of workers are needed in the organization, and at what salary.

Exercise 4

Which of the following does the HR department, or personnel department, deal with?

a. career development

b. recruitment

c. mail delivery

d. training

e. payments to suppliers

f. induction

g. discipline

Mini Webquest

- Find out how the human resource planning process needs to fit in with overall business strategy.

TOPIC 6.2 Recruitment

Recruitment is the business of recruiting or hiring people to work for a company. Usually this is managed by the Human Resources or Personnel department.

See also
Topic 6.1 **human resources, personnel**

hire

(hires, hiring, hired)

VERB

If you **hire** someone, you employ them or pay them to do a particular job for you.

The rest of the staff have been hired on short-term contracts.

recruitment consultant

(recruitment consultants)

N-COUNT

A **recruitment consultant** is a person or service that helps professional people to find work by introducing them to potential employers.

Recruitment consultants are a great way to find out what is going on.

You can also refer to a recruitment consultant as a **headhunter**.

headhunt

(headhunts, headhunting, headhunted)

VERB

If someone who works for a particular company **is headhunted**, they leave that company because another company has approached them and offered them another job with better pay and higher status.

They may headhunt her for the position of Executive Producer.

recruitment

N-UNCOUNT

COLLOCATIONS

a **recruitment** – consultancy / agency / specialist / drive / campaign / fair

reference

(references)

N-COUNT

A **reference** is a letter that is written by someone who knows you and that describes your character and abilities. When you apply for a job, an employer might ask for references.

The firm offered to give her a reference.

recruit

(recruits, recruiting, recruited)

VERB

If you **recruit** people for an organization, you select them and persuade them to join it or work for it.

Some organizations employ outside agencies to recruit staff for them, especially for managerial jobs.

CV

(CVs)

N-COUNT

Your **CV** is a brief written account of your personal details, your education and the jobs that you have had. You can send a CV when you are applying for a job. CV is an abbreviation for 'curriculum vitae'. [mainly BRIT]

Send them a copy of your CV.

In American English, use **résumé**.

referee

(referees)

N-COUNT

A **referee** is a person who gives you a reference, for example when you are applying for a job.

He was one of my referees when I successfully applied for the position.

probationary

ADJ

A **probationary** period is a period after someone starts a job, during which their employer can decide whether the person is suitable and should be allowed to continue.

At the end of the probationary period, you will become a permanent employee.

TASKS

Exercise 1

Put the following steps in the recruitment process in the correct order.

The recruitment process:	
a. the shortlisted candidates are interviewed ->	**1.** ______________
b. the candidates are interviewed ->	**2.** ______________
c. the successful candidate is offered the post.	**3.** ______________
d. individuals apply for the post in writing ->	**4.** ______________
e. the employer selects candidates for second interview ->	**5.** ______________
f. The post or position is advertised ->	**6.** ______________
g. the employer selects job candidates for first interview ->	**7.** ______________

Exercise 2

Use the terms in the box to complete the sentences below.

reference	hire	résumé
probationary	CV	recruit

If you **(a)**______________ or **(b)**______________ someone, you employ them or pay them to do a particular job for you.

A **(c)**______________ is a letter that is written by someone who has worked with you to your prospective employer and that describes your character and abilities.

A **(d)**______________ or **(e)**______________ is a brief written account of your personal details, your education and the jobs that you have had until now.

New recruits to a company will often work a **(f)**______________ period before their job contract is confirmed.

Exercise 3

Read the following online job advertisement and answer the questions that follow.

> Management Trainee (Customer Service)
>
> London
>
> We are one of the biggest telecoms companies in Europe, and we're recruiting Trainee Managers in London NOW. Join our Management Training Programme and we'll develop your talents for sales and customer service. Six month probationary period after training. To upload your CV and a reference, just click on the APPLY button below.
>
> APPLY

1. What positions are this company recruiting for?
2. Where are these positions based?
3. What skills will the company's training programme help to develop?
4. How long is their probationary period after training?
5. What two items should you upload if you want to apply?

Reflection

How important do you think a CV or résumé is to employers?
Have you ever used the services of a recruitment consultant?

TOPIC 6.3

Leaving a company

There are many different reasons why employees leave a company. On the one hand, they may decide to leave themselves because they want to move to another job or retire. On the other hand, they may be forced to leave their job by the company.

unfair dismissal

N-UNCOUNT

If an employee claims **unfair dismissal**, they begin legal action against their employer in which they claim that they were dismissed from their job unfairly.

They are claiming unfair dismissal at a tribunal.

fire

(fires, firing, fired)

VERB

If your employers **fire** you, they tell you that you can no longer work for them.

He has fired staff and cut costs, restoring profits.

give someone notice

PHRASE

If an employer **gives** an employee **notice**, the employer tells the employee that he or she must leave his or her job within a fixed period of time.

They were given 28 days' notice to leave their jobs.

hand in your notice

PHRASE

If you **hand in** your **notice**, you tell your employer that you intend to leave your job soon within a fixed period of time.

Two of the company's executives have handed in their notice.

You can also use **give in** your **notice**.

dismissal

N-UNCOUNT

COLLOCATIONS

wrongful / unfair / instant / constructive / controversial — **dismissal**

get the sack

PHRASE

If someone **gets the sack**, they are told that they can no longer work for their employer. [BRIT]

After four months I got the sack.

severance

N-UNCOUNT

Severance is a sum of money that a company gives to its employees when it has to stop employing them.

Workers will be given 60 days' notice and paid severance based on length of service.

Severance can also be called **severance pay**, **redundancy**, or **redundancy pay**.

dismiss

(dismisses, dismissing, dismissed)

VERB

When an employer **dismisses** an employee, the employer tells the employee that they are no longer needed to do the job they have been doing.

If you think you have been unfairly dismissed, you can complain to an industrial tribunal.

sack

(sacks, sacking, sacked)

VERB

If your employers **sack** you, they tell you that you can no longer work for them. [BRIT]

Nine more staff were sacked this week.

give someone the sack

PHRASE

If someone **is given the sack**, they are told that they can no longer work for their employer. [BRIT]

The workers were given the sack last week.

redundant

ADJ

If you are made **redundant**, your employer tells you to leave because your job is no longer necessary or because your employer cannot afford to keep paying you.

The software giant is to make 270 staff redundant in the UK.

TASKS

Exercise 1

Read the text and answer the questions that follow.

If an employer dismisses an employee, they make them leave their job. This is most likely because the employee has done something wrong. In many countries employers have to go through a set of legal procedures before firing someone: for example first warning, second warning, final warning, and then dismissal. On the other hand, if an employee is made redundant, their employer makes them leave their job because that role is no longer necessary or because the employer cannot afford to keep paying the employee. Redundancy terms are the conditions of redundancy, for example, the payment of a lump sum of money or keeping a pension.

1. If an employer dismisses someone, what do they make that person do?
2. Give two words from the opposite page that have the same meaning as 'dismiss'.
3. Why do employers make employees redundant?
4. What might be included in a company's redundancy terms?

Exercise 2

Which of the actions below are carried out by an employer and which by an employee? Complete the table.

	Employee	Employer
1. giving somebody notice to leave	☐	☐
2. handing in your notice	☐	☐
3. giving in your notice	☐	☐
4. making someone redundant	☐	☐
5. receiving severance pay	☐	☐
6. getting the sack	☐	☐
7. giving someone the sack	☐	☐
8. claiming unfair dismissal	☐	☐
9. firing someone	☐	☐

Exercise 3

When a worker is made redundant, the firm is obliged to make a payment to the employee. What is this payment called?

a. compensation

b. severance

Mini Webquest

- Find out about the legal redundancy and severance terms in different countries. How well are employees protected by the state in different countries in comparison to your own?

TOPIC 6.4 Remuneration

Remuneration is the formal term given to pay – the money that you get for work that you do.

salary
(salaries)

N-COUNT

A **salary** is the money that someone is paid each month by their employer, especially when they are skilled workers or are in a profession (for example teaching, law, medicine, business, media or banking).

Staff are paid a monthly salary.

performance-related pay

N-UNCOUNT

Performance-related pay is a rate of pay that is based on how well someone does their job.

The workers are free to choose between performance-related pay or their existing wage structure.

benefit
(benefits)

N-COUNT

Benefits are extra things that some people get from their job in addition to their salary, for example a car.

TCS offers employees a fairly comprehensive benefits package that includes stock options, health insurance and a pension scheme, as well as gym membership.

You can also call benefits **fringe benefits**.

income
(incomes)

N-VAR

A person's **income** is the money that they earn or receive, as opposed to the money that they have to spend or pay out.

Annual incomes are generally much lower here than in the capital.

payroll
(payrolls)

N-COUNT

The people on the **payroll** of a company or an organization are the people who work for it and are paid by it.

We provide services for overseas companies such as payroll processing and help desk operations.

remuneration

N-VAR

COLLOCATIONS

performance-based / total **remuneration**

a remuneration package / scheme

A **remuneration package** describes the total package for an employee: **salary**, **pension**, **benefits**, **share options** and **bonuses**.

bonus
(bonuses)

N-COUNT

A **bonus** is an extra amount of money that is added to someone's pay, usually because they have worked very hard.

We receive a substantial part of our pay in the form of bonuses.

wage
(wages)

N-COUNT

Wages are the amount of money that is regularly paid to workers for the work that they do.

The work is hazardous and the wages low.

pension
(pensions)

N-COUNT

Someone who has a **pension** receives a regular sum of money from the state or from a former employer because they have retired or because they are widowed or disabled.

There are at least as many types of company pension schemes as there are companies.

share option
(share options)

N-COUNT

A **share option** is an opportunity for the employees of a company to buy shares in the company at a special price. [BRIT]

Some firms offer share option schemes to all their employees.

In American English, use **stock option**.

TASKS

Exercise 1

Use the terms in the box to complete the paragraph.

bonuses	*pension*	*benefits*	*salary*
remuneration	*share options*	*performance-related*	*payroll*

A **(a)**________________ package is the total amount of money and extra things that an employee receives for the work that they do. If an employee is on a company's **(b)**________________, they work for and are paid by the company. In addition to their basic **(c)**________________, they may receive **(d)**________________, for example a car or medical care. They may also receive extra amounts of money, or **(e)**________________. This is especially true when they are receiving **(f)**________________ pay, which is a rate of pay based on how well someone does their job. Some companies also offer their staff **(g)**________________, or stock options, which means that they can buy shares in the company at a special price. Staff may also receive a **(h)**________________, which is money paid to an employee after they retire, for example at the age of 65.

Exercise 2

Which of the following are examples of fringe benefits?

1. stock options
2. rapid promotion
3. free health insurance
4. overseas travel on company business
5. use of a subsidized canteen
6. relocation package to cover moving expenses
7. company car
8. attendance at board meetings
9. being on the company payroll
10. company mobile phone

Exercise 3

Which of the following two employees do you think is most likely to prefer performance-related pay?

1. Keith is 42 years old, married with 3 small children. He's been with the firm for 12 years. He's good at his job, but he has never applied for a promotion and he has a poor sick-leave record.
2. Carolina is 26. She's just joined the firm on its new fast-track graduate program. She's single, often puts in unpaid extra work and loves travelling.

Reflection

What kind of remuneration package does your current job offer you?
What extra benefits would you like your company to offer you?

TOPIC 6.5

Industrial relations

The term 'industrial relations' refers to the relationship between employers and employees in industry, and the political decisions and laws that affect it.

trade union
(trade unions)

N-COUNT

A **trade union** is an organization that has been formed by workers in order to represent their rights and interests to their employers, for example in order to improve working conditions or wages. [mainly BRIT]

In Britain, trade union recognition is mandatory where employees want it.

You can also call a trade union a **trades union**. In American English, usually use **labor union**.

arbitration

N-UNCOUNT

Arbitration is the judging of a dispute between people or groups by someone who is not involved.

The matter is likely to go to arbitration.

grievance procedure
(grievance procedures)

N-COUNT

A **grievance procedure** is a set of guidelines produced by a company or organization, which explains how to make a formal complaint against them.

We have a formal grievance procedure in place to deal with staff complaints.

works council
(works councils)

N-COUNT

A **works council** is an elected body of workers within a company which negotiates with management over such things as working conditions, holiday and safety.

Employees failed to turn up because their works council refused to agree overtime.

industrial action

N-UNCOUNT

If workers take **industrial action**, they join together and do something to show that they are unhappy with their pay or working conditions, for example refusing to work.

They will decide next week whether to take industrial action over staffing levels.

go on strike

PHRASE

When workers **go on strike**, they stop doing their work for a period of time, usually in order to try to get better pay or conditions for themselves.

Staff at the hospital went on strike in protest at the incidents.

staff representative
(staff representatives)

N-COUNT

A **staff representative** is a worker who is elected by other workers to represent their interests to management.

The company must elect staff representatives to fulfil the legal requirements for consultation.

You can also refer to a staff representative as a **staff rep**.

tribunal
(tribunals)

N-COUNT

A **tribunal** is a special court or committee that is appointed to deal with particular problems.

His case comes before an industrial tribunal in March.

strike
(strikes, striking, struck)

N-COUNT

When there is a **strike**, workers stop doing their work for a period of time, usually in order to try to get better pay or conditions for themselves.

French air traffic controllers have begun a three-day strike in a dispute over pay.

VERB

When workers **strike**, they take part in a **strike**.

Workers have voted to strike in protest at the planned outsourcing deal.

TASKS

Exercise 1

Use the terms in the box to complete the paragraph.

industrial action	*arbitration*	*staff representatives*	*strike*	*works council*
tribunal	*trade union*	*grievance*	*industrial relations*	

Management and trade unions are jointly responsible for **(a)**____________________. In many companies, **(b)**____________________ are elected to form a **(c)**____________________, which negotiates with management over working conditions. If staff and management cannot resolve an issue together, they may use outside **(d)**____________________ to assist them. If all attempts to find a solution fail, the **(e)**____________________ may call a **(f)**____________________, or take other forms of **(g)**____________________. If an individual employee has a complaint, a company usually has a **(h)**____________________ procedure to deal with it. Employees may also contact their trade union or an industrial **(i)**____________________ if they have a complaint about their treatment at work or about a colleague.

Exercise 2

Read the text and answer the questions.

A recent EU directive requires every employer with more than 150 staff to establish a works council. Businesses will have statutory requirements for ongoing consultation on any proposed changes in working conditions, and to provide information about recent and probable developments and activities and about the establishment's economic situation.

1. What will companies with more than 150 employees have to do?
2. What will businesses be obliged to consult their workers about?
3. What two types of information will businesses be obliged to give their workers?

Exercise 3

When an employee begins a job they will sign a written contract of employment with the company, stating the conditions of work that have been agreed. Look at the list of conditions and put them under the correct heading.

NUMBER OF HOURS	TYPE OF EMPLOYMENT	PAY	BENEFITS	DISCIPLINARY PROCEDURES	NOTICE	GRIEVANCE PROCEDURES	EMPLOYEE RIGHTS

a. 4 weeks paid holiday per year
b. paid sick leave
c. 48 hours per week
d. one month's notice
e. consequences of breaking company rules
f. who to contact to make a complaint
g. £20,000 per year
h. $9 per hour
i. trade union membership
j. permanent/temporary job
k. full time/part time

Reflection

How important do you think trade unions or works councils are?
Do you think that strikes are effective in industrial relations?

TOPIC 6.6 Equal opportunities

The term 'equal opportunities' refers to the policy of giving everyone the same opportunities for employment, pay and promotion, without discriminating against particular groups.

discriminate

(discriminates, discriminating, discriminated)

VERB

To **discriminate** against a group of people or in favour of a group of people means to unfairly treat them worse or better than other groups.

They believe the law discriminates against women.

age discrimination

N-UNCOUNT

Age discrimination is the practice of treating older people less fairly or less well than other people.

He was told that he was too old, and he sued for age discrimination.

racial discrimination

N-UNCOUNT

Racial discrimination is the practice of treating people of some races less fairly or less well than those of another race.

A tribunal found GMP guilty of racial discrimination.

under-represented

ADJ

If a group of people is **under-represented** in a particular activity, there are fewer of them involved in the activity than you think there should be.

Women are still under-represented in top-level civil service jobs.

equal opportunities

N-PLURAL

COLLOCATIONS

an equal opportunities policy / employer / legislation

diversity and equal opportunities

to promote equal opportunities

disability

(disabilities)

N-COUNT

A **disability** is a permanent injury, illness, or physical or mental condition that tends to restrict the way that someone can live their life.

Facilities for people with disabilities are still insufficient.

discrimination

N-UNCOUNT

Discrimination is the practice of treating one person or group of people less fairly or less well than other people or groups.

The legislation prohibits discrimination against individuals on the grounds of sexual orientation.

sexual discrimination

N-UNCOUNT

Sexual discrimination is the practice of treating the members of one sex, usually women, less fairly or less well than those of the other sex.

Her complaint against the company for sexual discrimination was upheld by a tribunal.

positive discrimination

N-UNCOUNT

Positive discrimination means making sure that people such as women, members of smaller racial groups, and disabled people get a fair share of the opportunities available. [BRIT]

I am all for diversity but I am not in favour of positive discrimination.

You can also talk about **positive action**. In American English, use **affirmative action**.

TASKS

Exercise 1

Use the terms in the box to complete the paragraph.

discriminated against	*under-represented*	*disability*
equal opportunities	*positive action*	*equal opportunities monitoring*

When a company interviews a candidate for a job, they are not allowed to discriminate against him or her on the grounds of race, sex, age or **(a)**____________________. In other words every candidate should have **(b)**____________________, or the same chance to get the job. EU laws help to promote this, as do other laws in other parts of the world. Figures suggest that candidates are often discriminated against on the grounds of race. Many people believe that **(c)**____________________ by employers is an important part of a good equal opportunities policy. This should help to increase the number of workers belonging to a particular racial group, if they are **(d)**____________________ in the firm. Firms need to be aware of the makeup of their labour force, and many companies carry out **(e)**____________________ during the selection procedure. As well as discrimination in the selection process, employees can also be discriminated against in the area of pay. In manufacturing, for example, women earn 72% of men's pay. Additionally, occupations that employ mainly women, such as hairdressing for example, tend to involve low pay. If an employee thinks that they have been **(f)**____________________ they can take their case to an industrial tribunal.

Exercise 2

Look at the two tables showing employment trends in one country and answer the questions.

A. Percentage of the workforce by gender and occupation

	Men		Women	
Area of employment	**Year 1**	**Year 5**	**Year 1**	**Year 5**
Managers	16	19	8	12
Professional	11	13	8	9
Clerical	8	8	31	25
Manufacturing	25	17	4	3

B. Unemployment by ethnic groups

Ethnic Group	% Unemployment
White	5
Black	21
Asian	9
Others	14
Country average	7

1. According to the information in the tables:
  - **a.** Has discrimination against women in management increased or decreased?
  - **b.** Do men and women have equal opportunities to gain employment in the manufacturing sector?
  - **c.** Is there any sexual discrimination in the clerical sector?
  - **d.** Which ethnic group suffers the worst racial discrimination in employment?
  - **e.** Which ethnic group has the highest level of employment?

2. If far-reaching programmes of compulsory positive discrimination were introduced, what trends might be seen in the tables above:
  - **a.** in the manufacturing sector?
  - **b.** among black workers?
  - **c.** among managers?

Mini Webquest

- Find out about any large organization's recruitment policy.
- Find out more about positive discrimination, positive action or affirmative action.

TOPIC 7.1

Management

A company's management philosophy is the set of ideas that it has about how the business should be run.

motivate
(motivates, motivating, motivated)

VERB

If you are **motivated** by something, especially an emotion, it causes you to behave in a particular way.

They are motivated by a need to achieve.

management consultant
(management consultants)

N-COUNT

A **management consultant** is someone whose job is to advise companies on the most efficient ways to run their business, especially companies that are not performing very well.

Only after a management consultant visited the office was a solution to the problem found.

supervise
(supervises, supervising, supervised)

VERB

If you **supervise** an activity or person, you make sure that the activity is done correctly or that the person is doing a task or behaving correctly.

An engineer supervised the construction of the buildings.

motivated
ADJ

Someone who is **motivated** has a strong wish to do something.

We have highly motivated employees.

management
N-UNCOUNT

COLLOCATIONS

management – strategy / style / structure / expertise / consultancy / techniques

responsibility
N-UNCOUNT

If someone is given **responsibility**, they are given the right or opportunity to make important decisions or to take action without having to get permission from anyone else.

Give staff responsibility and the ability to make decisions, which will facilitate autonomy and freedom.

theory X
N-UNCOUNT

Theory X is the idea that employees work better when they are closely supervised and when their work is strictly controlled.

Theory X reflects an underlying belief that management must counteract an inherent human tendency to avoid work.

theory Y
N-UNCOUNT

Theory Y is the idea that employees work better when they are given responsibility for their own work and when their personal needs are satisfied.

Theory Y is a participative style of management which assumes that people will exercise self-direction and self-control.

Theory X and Y were based on *Maslow's hierarchy of needs* which showed how workers could be motivated to perform better in their jobs if their higher needs for personal satisfaction were met.

Abraham Maslow was a psychologist who first presented his ideas in the 1940s. Theory X and Y were ideas that were developed by Douglas McGregor at the Massachusetts Institute of Technology in the USA in the 1960s.

TASKS

Exercise 1

Use the terms in the box to complete the paragraph.

theory X	*responsibility*	*management consultants*	*motivated*
supervised	*motivates*	*theory Y*	

Different management philosophies take different views about what **(a)**__________________ employees. The idea that employees work better when they are closely **(b)**__________________ is known as **(c)**__________________. The idea that employees work better when they are given **(d)**__________________ for their own work is known as **(e)**__________________. According to Theory Y, a well-**(f)**__________________ worker is more likely to work hard. Some companies employ **(g)**__________________ who offer advice and support in order to help improve performance.

Exercise 2

Theory X and theory Y are management philosophies that describe the reasons why people work, based on opposing views of people's motivation. Put the reasons into the correct place in the table.

1. Workers can enjoy work.
2. Workers are selfish, ignore the needs of organizations, avoid responsibility and lack ambition.
3. Management should create a situation where workers can show creativity and apply their knowledge to the job.
4. Workers are motivated by money.

Theory X	Theory Y
	Workers have many different needs which motivate them.
Workers are lazy and dislike work.	
	If motivated, workers can organize themselves and take responsibility.
Workers need to be controlled and directed by management.	

Mini Webquest

- Find out more about *Maslow's hierarchy of needs.*

Reflection

What do you think makes a good manager?
What do you think makes a bad manager?

TOPIC 7.2 Management styles

A person's management style is the way that they behave as a manager. Some managers will have a very autocratic style of management and make all the key decisions without asking for anyone else's advice or input, while other managers will have a democratic style of management.

autocratic

ADJ

An **autocratic** person or organization has complete power and makes decisions without asking anyone else's advice.

Weston's autocratic style at the family firm had its critics.

laissez-faire

ADJ

A **laissez-faire** style or approach is based on the idea that people should be allowed to make decisions themselves, without interference from those in authority.

Technically, we have laissez-faire management - we all talk a lot over the Internet about what we might do.

democratic

ADJ

Something that is **democratic** is based on the idea that everyone should have equal rights and should be involved in making important decisions.

She's quite democratic in that she'll listen to ideas from anybody really.

hands-on

ADJ

A **hands-on** approach involves making decisions and doing things yourself, rather than just talking about them or getting someone else to do them.

She has always taken a hands-on approach to quality control.

delegate

(delegates, delegating, delegated)

VERB

If you **delegate** duties, responsibilities or power to someone, you give them those duties, those responsibilities or that power so that they can act on your behalf.

Many employers find it hard to delegate.

A person's management style will depend on:

- their personality
- their training
- their experience
- the culture of the organization that they are in

hands-off

ADJ

A **hands-off** style or approach is based on the idea that people should be allowed to make decisions themselves, without interference from those in authority.

The CEO prefers a hands-off approach.

collaborative

ADJ

A **collaborative** piece of work is done by two or more people or groups working together.

We have a more collaborative approach to management than some of the more hierarchical management styles.

culture

(cultures)

N-COUNT

The **culture** of a particular organization or group consists of the habits of the people in it and the way that they generally behave.

We find that a culture of openness leads to thoughtful and creative work.

decision-making

N-UNCOUNT

Decision-making is the process of reaching decisions, especially in a large organization or in government.

Management decision-making in a democratic culture may be sluggish.

TASKS

Exercise 1

Put these three terms into the correct place in the table:

1. laissez-faire **2.** democratic **3.** autocratic

management style	method
a.	Leader makes decisions. Others are informed and carry them out.
b.	Leader discusses with others before the decision is made. The group can influence the decision that is made.
c.	There is no formal structure to make decisions. The leader does not force his or her views on others.

Exercise 2

Choose the correct answer to each question.

1. Which two of these leaders are least likely to delegate responsibility?
 a. an autocratic leader
 b. a hands-on leader
 c. a laissez-faire leader

2. Which of these leaders is most likely to involve staff in collective decision-making?
 a. an autocratic leader
 b. a democratic leader
 c. a laissez-faire leader

3. Which two of these leaders are most likely to leave decision-making to individual members of staff?
 a. an autocratic leader
 b. a hands-off leader
 c. a laissez-faire leader

Exercise 3

Read the text about management ability and answer the questions.

A good manager should look after, motivate, develop and empower their staff. They should also be able to identify the training needs of their staff. Good managers regularly monitor and review the performance of their staff. Setting measurable and achievable objectives is an important way of ensuring that staff remain motivated.

1. Who should a good manager look after and develop?

2. What should a good manager be able to identify?

3. What do good managers regularly do?

4. Why is it important to set measurable and achievable objectives?

Reflection

What style of management have the managers you have worked with had?

TOPIC 7.3

Management roles

Managers have many different roles in their day-to-day working lives, from leading a team or department to carrying out performance appraisals and recommending promotions. Providing leadership is the main role of a manager.

See also
Topic 8.3 **appraisal**

promotion
(promotions)
N-VAR

If you are given **promotion** or a **promotion** in your job, you are given a more important job or rank in the organization that you work for.

He was very career-minded and had been recommended for promotion early.

leadership
N-UNCOUNT

Leadership refers to the qualities that make someone a good leader, or the methods that a leader uses to do his or her job.

What most people want to see is determined, decisive action and firm leadership.

lead
(leads, leading, led)
VERB

If you **lead** a group of people, an organization or an activity, you are in control or in charge of the people, the organization or the activity.

The agency is led by a management team of 15 people.

line manager
(line managers)
N-COUNT

Your **line manager** is the person at work who is in charge of your department, group or project.

Speak to your line manager and ask if there are any opportunities to move up or even sideways.

Management roles:

- directing
- assessing performance – praising, criticizing, recommending, asking, telling
- planning
- organizing
- communicating information

report
(reports, reporting, reported)
VERB

If you say that one employee **reports** to another, you mean that the first employee is told what to do by the second one who is responsible for them.

Individuals report to project managers who control specific projects.

flat
ADJ

Companies with a **flat** structure are organized in a less hierarchical way than traditional companies, with the aim of giving all employees a relatively equal status within the company.

The management structure remains flat rather than hierarchical to make everyone feel they have an important role to play.

In a flat structure, important decisions and changes can usually be made faster.

hierarchical
ADJ

A **hierarchical** system or organization is one in which people have different ranks or positions, depending on how important they are.

They claim that the hierarchical structure of schools replicates the hierarchical structure of the workplace.

TASKS

Exercise 1

Use the terms in the box to complete the sentences.

promotion	*report*	*organizing*	*leadership*	*line manager*

1. A ________________ is someone who has responsibility for managing other employees.
2. Staff ________________ to their line manager.
3. A good manager demonstrates strong ________________ skills.
4. Directing, planning and ________________ are all part of the role of a manager.
5. Managers may recommend the________________ of their best employees.

Exercise 2

Which type of workplace relationship, shown by the diagrams, is most likely to include line managers?

HIERARCHICAL STRUCTURE

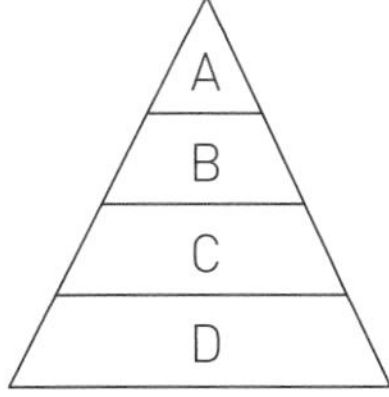

FLAT STRUCTURE

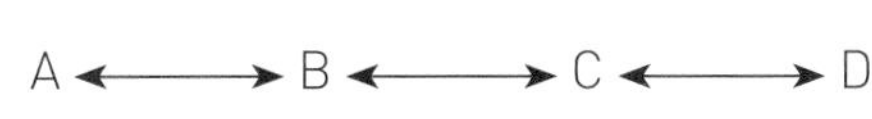

Exercise 3

Look at this organizational chart and answer the questions below.

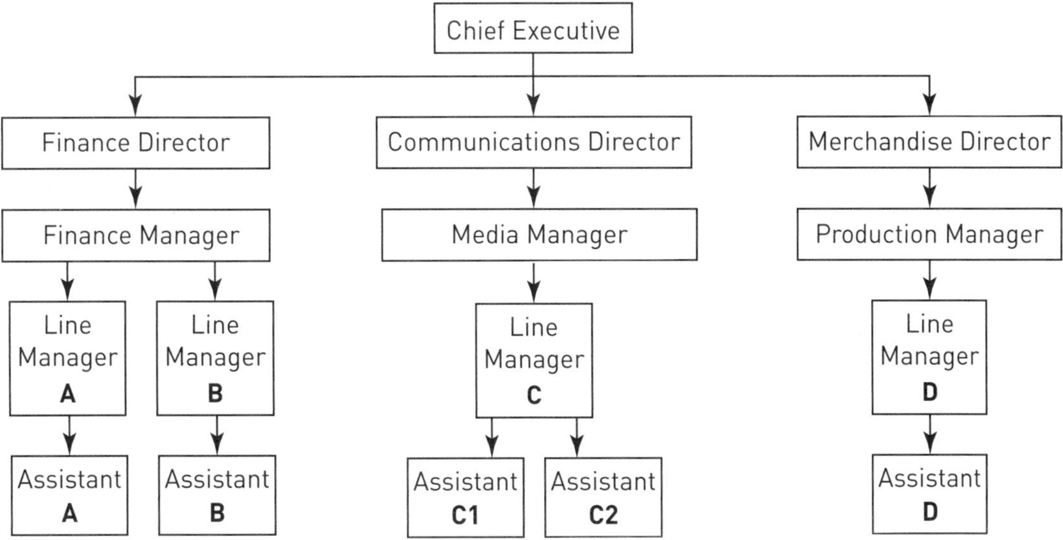

1. How many people report directly to the Chief Executive?
2. How many Managers report directly to each Director?
3. How many Line Managers report to the Finance Manager?
4. How many Assistants are in the team led by Line Manager C?
5. Who does Assistant D report to?
6. Does this organization have a flat or hierarchical structure?

Mini Webquest

- Find out about **Mintzberg's 10 Management Roles**.
- Find out about **Matrix Management**.

Reflection

What do you think is the most important role for a manager?

TOPIC 7.4 Change management

Change management is a style and process of management that aims to encourage organizations and individuals to deal effectively with the changes taking place in their work. Often this involves restructuring the business.

restructure

(restructures, restructuring, restructured)

VERB

To **restructure** an organization or system means to change the way in which it is organized, usually in order to make it work more effectively.

I've restructured the company around our core markets: consumer goods and retail.

reassure

(reassures, reassuring, reassured)

VERB

If you **reassure** someone, you say or do things to make them stop worrying about something.

All 650 staff at the factory have been reassured that their jobs are safe.

stakeholder

(stakeholders)

N-COUNT

Stakeholders are people who have an interest in a company's or organization's affairs.

You have to involve and seek the agreement of all the stakeholders and interested parties.

crisis management

N-UNCOUNT

People use **crisis management** to refer to a management style that concentrates on solving the immediate problems occurring in a business rather than looking for long-term solutions.

This isn't an investment strategy; it is crisis management.

consult

(consults, consulting, consulted)

VERB

If a person or group of people **consults** with other people or **consults** them, they talk and exchange ideas and opinions about what they might decide to do.

We've consulted extensively with key stakeholders.

Steps in change management:

identify what needs to be changed

↓

describe what needs to be changed

↓

make suggestions for changes

↓

consult the stakeholders – customers, workers, managers – about possible changes

↓

refine plans for change

↓

implement change

↓

cement change

thrive

(thrives, thriving, thrived)

VERB

If you say that someone **thrives** on a particular situation, you mean that they enjoy it or that they can deal with it very well, especially when other people find it unpleasant or difficult.

Some people thrive on change.

VERB

If a business or businessperson **thrives**, they do well and are successful.

The business has thrived, despite the recession.

threatened

ADJ

If you feel **threatened**, you feel as if someone is trying to harm you.

Threatened by change, we fight to maintain the status quo, often to our detriment.

TASKS

Exercise 1

Use the terms in the box to complete the paragraph.

consult	*threatened*	*thrive*	*crisis management*
restructuring	*change management*	*reassure*	*stakeholders*

(a)________________ is the process of dealing effectively with changes taking place in the workplace. This can involve **(b)**________________ a business to deal with changes in the market place. Sometimes individuals in organizations are afraid of change because they feel **(c)**________________ and insecure in their roles. Managers will usually try to **(d)**________________ them. However, other individuals **(e)**________________ on change. It is part of a manager's role to **(f)**________________ with **(g)**________________ about the changes. Change management usually involves long-term planning, but sometimes **(h)**________________ is used to resolve immediate problems, for example when a company is going bankrupt.

Exercise 2

Does the speaker in each sentence **thrive** *on change or feel* **threatened** *by change?*

1. When my company announced that it was restructuring, I was afraid that I might lose my job.
2. I enjoy adapting my skills to suit the needsof the business – it keeps my work interesting.
3. I think it would be boring if nothing ever changed – it always feels good to move forward.
4. I'm not confident about learning new skills – I'd rather stick with one role for life.

Exercise 3

Match the two halves of each sentence.

1. Crisis management has	**a.** feel confident enough to expand overseas.
2. BW now plans to spend the next few months consulting with	**b.** until it has consulted all stakeholders.
3. Businesses have restructured and now	**c.** replaced strategic thinking.
4. The council voted to defer a decision	**d.** its stakeholders and customers to get their reactions to its proposals.

Mini Webquest

- Find out about **Lewin's three-stage change management process.**

Reflection

What is your attitude to change?
Do you feel threatened by it or do you thrive on it?

TOPIC 8.1 Career paths

Your career path or progression is the direction that your career takes you from your first job to retirement. In the past many people had jobs for life, but these days they often have more than one career and have to retrain.

drive

N-UNCOUNT

If you say that someone has **drive**, you mean that they have energy and determination.

Often the business start up skills of drive, determination and self-belief can see the business through the early stages.

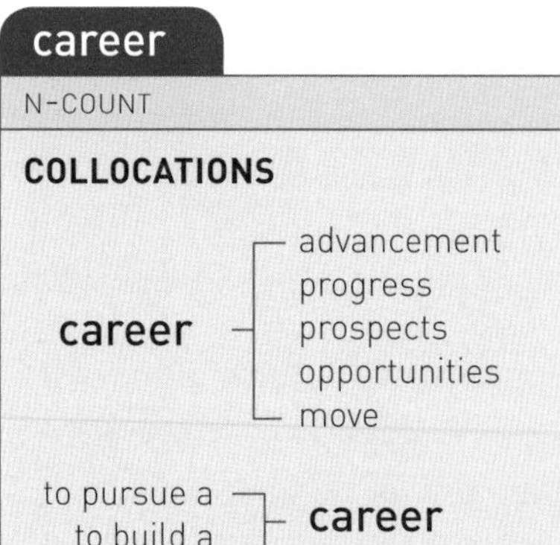

skill

(skills)

N-COUNT

A **skill** is a type of work or activity that requires special training and knowledge.

Many skills are easily transferable and are valued by a new employer.

networking

N-UNCOUNT

Networking is the process of trying to meet new people who might be useful to you in your job, often through social activities.

Several business networking sites enable you to find customers that are looking for your services or products.

Your career path will depend on:

- opportunities for promotion within the organization
- job opportunities in competing companies
- your drive or ambition
- luck, for example being in the right place at the right time
- your qualifications
- your skills and competencies
- your interests
- your knowledge
- your location, networking skills and contacts

contact

(contacts)

N-COUNT

A **contact** is someone that you know in an organization or profession who helps you or gives you information.

I used my skills as a chef and my contacts in the restaurant business to arrange the event.

retraining

N-UNCOUNT

Retraining is the process of learning new skills, especially in order to get a new job.

A lot of people are going to face job loss and are going to need job retraining.

Changing your career path may require:

- retraining
- improving your skills
- moving to another company
- building up your CV or résumé
- relocating to another city or town
- a sideways move

sideways

ADJ

If you make a **sideways** move in your work or career, you get a new job that is different, but at the same level.

Studying project management has enabled me to make a sideways move into IT, which has been less affected by the economic downturn.

TASKS

Exercise 1

Use the terms in the box to complete the paragraph.

skills	*contacts*	*career path*	*sideways*
retraining	*drive*	*networking*	

The direction that your career takes you from your first job to retirement is called your **(a)**____________________. Nowadays people often have more than one career and need **(b)**____________________ to help them learn new **(c)**____________________. As well as their skills and competencies, a person's career path may be affected by their **(d)**____________________ or ambition, their **(e)**____________________ skills and the **(f)**____________________ or people they know. Changing your career path might involve making a **(g)**____________________ move to a different job.

Exercise 2

Read the text and answer the questions.

> At the beginning of your career you may need to get unpaid or paid work experience in a company as an intern. Your career path may involve a sideways move into something different, or you may decide to retrain to learn new skills. At the end of your career, and possibly after you have retired, you may work part-time, for example a couple of days a week or month.

1. When might you need to work as an intern?

2. When might you work part-time?

3. Why might you decide to retrain?

4. What kind of move might your career path involve?

Exercise 3

Match the information taken from a CV with the correct heading.

QUALIFICATIONS	**a.** Windows, Word, Excel, British Certificate of Multi-media Computing
EMPLOYMENT	**b.** Flexibility, problem-solving, good communication
TECHNICAL SKILLS	**c.** Technical Support Engineer AVS Ltd, Birmingham, Aug 2008-Aug 2011
PERSONAL SKILLS	**d.** ski-ing, swimming, online gaming, cinema
PERSONAL INTERESTS	**e.** 6 GCSEs at grade A; 4 A Levels at grade B
REFERENCES	**f.** Available on request

Mini Webquest

- Find and compare business networking sites.

Reflection

Draw a map of your career path to date and what you would like to be doing in 2, 5 and 10 years' time.

TOPIC 8.2 Business qualifications

Many people get business qualifications before they enter the world of work, but increasingly people improve their CVs by gaining business qualifications while they are at work. They may take unpaid leave or study after work in the evenings to gain these qualifications.

diploma
(diplomas)

N-COUNT

A **diploma** is a qualification that may be awarded to a student by a university or college, or by a high school in the United States.

I did a diploma in computer science at Birkbeck College.

specialism
(specialisms)

N-COUNT

A **specialism** is a specific area of knowledge or skill within a particular subject.

Universities offer different specialisms, such as medical or technical translating.

MBA
(MBAs)

N-COUNT

An **MBA** is a master's degree in business administration. You can also refer to a person who has this degree as an **MBA**. **MBA** is an abbreviation for 'Master of Business Administration'.

We prefer to hire MBAs who have an engineering background.

degree
N-COUNT

COLLOCATIONS

to earn a / an economics / a university / a three-year / an honours / a postgraduate / a masters — **degree**

a degree — in economics / in engineering / in mathematics / in accountancy

first degree
(first degrees)

N-COUNT

People who have gained a higher qualification after completing a basic university degree such as a BA or a BSc refer to that basic degree as their **first degree**.

A first degree in business takes about five years, and those wishing to study further are more likely to go straight to doctorates than study for a masters.

distance learning
N-UNCOUNT

Distance learning is the activity of studying at home and sending your work to a teacher in order to gain a qualification.

Part-time and distance learning MBAs are also options.

sponsor
(sponsors, sponsoring, sponsored)

VERB

If an organization or an individual **sponsors** something such as someone's training, they pay some or all of the expenses connected with it.

Some students have persuaded their employers to sponsor them.

apprenticeship
(apprenticeships)

N-VAR

Someone who has an **apprenticeship** works for a fixed period of time for a person who has a particular skill in order to learn the skill. **Apprenticeship** is the system of learning a skill like this.

He served an engineering apprenticeship with a large electrical manufacturer.

TASKS

Exercise 1

Use the terms in the box to complete the paragraph.

apprenticeships	*first degree*	*MBA*
sponsored	*specialisms*	*diploma*

People do **(a)**__________________ courses at university or college in subjects like Business Studies and Economics. These courses give them a BSc or BA degree. When people are in work, they may take a **(b)**__________________ or degree course to improve their skills and knowledge in a particular area, for example by doing a marketing diploma. People with managerial ambitions often do an **(c)**__________________ during the early part of their career after they have had some experience. The MBA course may be **(d)**__________________ by their company or they may have to pay for the course themselves. Many MBA programmes offer **(e)**__________________, for example in Marketing, Strategic Planning and Finance. **(f)**__________________ are when young people work for an individual or company and learn a particular skill, for example in engineering or IT.

Exercise 2

What kind of MBA is most suited to each person?

Types of MBA:

- **Full-time** MBA (generally one or two years)
- **Part-time** MBA (around two to three years)
- **Distance learning** MBA

a. Claire's employer has agreed to sponsor her MBA course if she continues to work for them at the same time.

b. Mohammed wants to get his MBA as quickly as possible and can afford to pay for it himself.

c. Ying looks after her young children at home. She'd like to study for an MBA, but wants to stay close to her family.

d. Steven works 3 days a week, but has 3 days he could spend studying for an MBA.

e. Adam lives outside the city and travel to the university is too expensive, so he'd prefer to study for his MBA from home.

Exercise 3

Match the two halves of the sentences.

1. The university offers

2. I completed a four-year apprenticeship and I am currently

3. MBA students may wish to

4. He gained a business

a. completing a national diploma in electrical engineering.

b. degree at Strathclyde University.

c. high-quality degrees through distance learning.

d. pursue a particular business specialism.

Mini Webquest

- Find out about the different types of MBA on offer in your country and in the USA.

Reflection

MBAs are hard work and expensive, so they can take up a lot of time and money. Do you think studying for an MBA is a good way to spend time and money?
Why/Why not?

TOPIC 8.3

Professional development and performance appraisal

One of the main purposes of performance appraisal is to identify training needs. A manager should discuss what kind of training would help improve performance. A performance appraisal is also about reviewing the past year's objectives and setting objectives for the next year.

objective
(objectives)

N-COUNT

Your **objective** is what you are trying to achieve.

Firms may promise promotions or bonuses based on achieving set objectives.

appraisal
(appraisals)

N-VAR

Appraisal is the official or formal assessment of the strengths and weaknesses of someone or something. **Appraisal** often involves observation or some kind of testing.

Staff problems should be addressed through training and appraisals.

In a business context, appraisals are often described as **performance appraisals** or **performance reviews**.

performance

N-VAR

COLLOCATIONS

performance – appraisal / indicator / bonus / evaluation / criteria / targets / review / rating / assessment / management

training

N-UNCOUNT

Training is the process of learning the skills that you need for a particular job or activity.

He called for much higher spending on education and training.

staff development

N-UNCOUNT

Staff development is the process of teaching the employees of a company new skills that will help them to advance in their job.

We place an emphasis on staff development and feel that it is vital for staff to continually update and improve their skills.

in-house

ADJ

In-house work or activities are done by employees of an organization or company, rather than by workers outside the organization or company.

A lot of companies do in-house training.

ADV

If work or activities are done **in-house**, they are done by employees of an organization or company, rather than by workers outside the organization or company.

The magazine is still produced in-house.

workshop
(workshops)

N-COUNT

A **workshop** is a period of discussion or practical work on a particular subject in which a group of people share their knowledge or experience.

The staff should attend a diversity workshop if they have not already.

role play
(role plays)

N-VAR

Role play is the act of imitating the character and behaviour of someone who is different from yourself, for example as a training exercise.

Group members have to communicate with each other through role play.

case study
(case studies)

N-COUNT

A **case study** is a written account that gives detailed information about a person, group or thing and their development over a period of time.

The programme offers both job-related and competency training, with case studies and assessments available online.

TASKS

Exercise 1

Use the terms in the box to complete the paragraph.

in-house	*role plays*	*case studies*
training	*workshop*	*staff development*

(a)________________ is the teaching of new skills to help staff to advance in their job. Companies often run **(b)**________________ training courses that focus on communication and day-to-day business skills. These **(c)**________________ courses will generally last one or two days. Usually courses are run as a **(d)**________________ with participants getting a lot of hands-on experience of doing things like taking part in **(e)**________________ and simulations, and discussing **(f)**________________.

Exercise 2

Who would benefit most from the following in-house training courses?

In-house training courses:

- **Negotiating**
- **Presenting**
- **Prioritizing / Time management**
- **Dealing with conflict**
- **Health & Safety in the workplace**
- **Using computers**
- **Project management**

1. Sam has worked as a Business Manager for many years, but his office has only recently started to use a computer database instead of paper files. Sam has little experience of working with computers.
2. Anya has just completed a First Aid course and wants to become the Safety Officer for her department.
3. Josh was recently promoted to become a line manager, but he finds it difficult to balance his time between his staff and his own workload.
4. Deepak has collaborated in many projects in the past, but he'd like to take on more responsibility, and perhaps start managing his own projects.
5. Chloe is a mentor and often has to deal with difficult situations that can involve conflict.
6. Angelo has created a new software programme and has been asked to give a presentation on it next month. But he is nervous about speaking to large groups of people.
7. Miryam works for a Purchasing Department and often has to negotiate a price with suppliers, but she'd like to improve her skills.

Exercise 3

Are the following sentences ***true*** *or* ***false****?*

1. A performance appraisal can also be called a performance review.
2. A performance appraisal involves discussing products.
3. It is usual to set objectives during a performance appraisal.
4. Reviewing past performance is part of most performance appraisals.
5. A performance appraisal helps to identify the training needs of staff.
6. Workshops and role play are often used during performance appraisals.

Reflection

If you could go on an in-house training course tomorrow, which course would you choose?

TOPIC 8.4 Learning organizations, mentoring and coaching

Companies often state that their most valuable asset is the people who work for them. Learning organizations are companies that facilitate the personal development of their staff, which benefits the development of the company.

See also
Topic 8.3 **training, staff development**

mentor
(mentors, mentoring, mentored)

N-COUNT

A person's **mentor** is someone who gives them help and advice over a period of time, especially help and advice related to their job.

You should seek on-the-job opportunities such as becoming a mentor or coach to other staff.

VERB

To **mentor** someone means to give them help and advice over a period of time, especially help and advice related to their job.

Graduate Trainees are mentored for the first year.

confidential

ADJ

Information that is **confidential** is meant to be kept secret or private.

Don't worry about filling in personal information: we keep it strictly confidential.

asset
(assets)

N-COUNT

Something or someone that is an **asset** is considered useful or helps a person or organization to be successful.

Our workers are our most valuable assets.

mentoring

N-UNCOUNT

Mentoring is the practice of assigning a junior member of staff to the care of a more experienced member of staff in order to provide the more junior employee with help and assistance.

Mentoring is crucial, especially as inexperienced new graduates can land senior positions.

mentor

N-COUNT

COLLOCATIONS

a mentor – coaches / supervises / guides / teaches / helps / encourages

coaching

N-UNCOUNT

Coaching is special training to help a person become better at a particular skill.

Managers offer coaching and guidance to help staff members fulfil their potential.

mentee
(mentees)

N-COUNT

A **mentee** is a person who receives help and advice from a mentor, especially help and advice related to their job.

So how does mentoring benefit the mentor and the mentee?

one-to-one

ADJ

In a **one-to one** situation or relationship, one person deals directly with another person.

We still do one-to-one training, but the online training has proven very successful.

facilitate
(facilitates, facilitating, facilitated)

VERB

To **facilitate** an action or process, especially one that you would like to happen, means to make it easier or more likely to happen.

Line managers need to help employees perform successfully in their roles and facilitate personal development.

TASKS

Exercise 1

Use the terms in the box to complete the paragraph.

confidential	*one-to-one*	*facilitate*	*mentored*
coaching	*mentee*	*asset*	*mentor*

Many organizations consider their staff to be their most valuable **(a)**____________________. When a person starts a new job or takes on a new role, the manager may appoint a **(b)**____________________ to give advice to that person. A mentor usually has a lot of experience. The person being **(c)**____________________ can ask questions about what to do in their new job or role without worrying about what their line manager might think. Usually the conversations between mentor and **(d)**____________________ are **(e)**____________________. **(f)**____________________ focuses on a specific need or situation and is often carried out by the line manager. For example, at a performance appraisal the person being appraised may say that they have a day-to-day problem, perhaps a difficulty communicating effectively with a customer. The line manager will then agree to help them with this problem and work **(g)**____________________ with them over the next four weeks to solve the problem. In this way, the line manager helps to **(h)**____________________ the development of their staff.

Exercise 2

Choose the correct answer.

1. *Who is more likely to be your mentor at work?*
  a. the Managing Director
  b. a new employee
  c. an experienced co-worker

2. *Who is more likely to be a mentee at work?*
  a. the Managing Director
  b. a new employee
  c. an experienced co-worker

3. *Which of the following is not likely to be involved in coaching?*
  a. the Managing Director
  b. a line manager
  c. a new employee

4. *Who is more likely to give coaching at work?*
  a. a line manager
  b. a new employee
  c. the Managing Director

Mini Webquest

- Find out about the origin of the concept **The Learning Organization**.

Reflection

What qualities do you think you need to be good at mentoring or coaching?
Do you think you would make a good mentor?

TOPIC 8.5 Leave

Leave is a period of time when you are not working at your job, because you are on holiday or on vacation, or for some other reason.

sick leave

N-UNCOUNT

Sick leave is the time that a person spends away from work because of illness or injury.

I have been on sick leave for three months with depression.

parental leave

N-UNCOUNT

Parental leave is a time away from work, usually without pay, that parents are allowed in order to look after their children.

Parents are entitled to 13 weeks' parental leave.

compassionate leave

N-UNCOUNT

Compassionate leave is time away from work that your employer allows you for personal reasons, especially when a member of your family dies or is seriously ill.

Staff are entitled to sick pay, compassionate leave and annual holidays.

absenteeism

N-UNCOUNT

Absenteeism is the fact or habit of frequently being away from work, usually without a good reason.

Happy employees have lower levels of absenteeism.

leave

N-UNCOUNT

COLLOCATIONS

to be on / annual / paid / unpaid / maternal / paternal – **leave**

leave – entitlement

stress

(stresses)

N-VAR

If you feel under **stress**, you feel worried and tense because of difficulties in your life or work.

Learning how to deal with stress is one of the most important ways to stay healthy.

sick building syndrome

N-UNCOUNT

Sick building syndrome is a group of conditions, including headaches, sore eyes and tiredness, which people who work in offices may experience because the air there is not healthy to breathe.

Some employees complained that the poor air ventilation had created sick building syndrome.

holiday

N-UNCOUNT

If you have a particular number of days' or weeks' **holiday**, you do not have to go to work for that number of days or weeks. [BRIT]

Every worker will be entitled to four weeks' paid holiday a year.

In American English, use **vacation**.

turnover

(turnovers)

N-VAR

The **turnover** of people in an organization or place is the rate at which people leave and are replaced.

Harassment can lead to increased absenteeism and stress, higher turnover of staff and decreased productivity.

TASKS

Exercise 1

Use the terms in the box to complete the paragraph.

stress	*sick building syndrome*	*sick leave*	*holiday*	*on leave*
parental leave	*turnover*	*absenteeism*	*compassionate leave*	

There are many different reasons for an employee to be **(a)**________________. If they are going on **(b)**________________ or vacation, they may take annual leave. If they are sick or unwell, then they may go on **(c)**________________. If they have young children, then they may go on **(d)**________________. If a family member is sick or has died, then they may be granted **(e)**________________ by their employer. **(f)**________________ may be the result of **(g)**________________ or depression. High levels of staff sickness in one place may be the result of poor air quality, or **(h)**________________. Poor job satisfaction often results in a high **(i)**________________ of staff, which can have considerable cost implications for a company.

Exercise 2

Look at the figures and answer the questions.

Sick leave taken in four comparable manufacturing companies – average from 4-year period.

Company	**Days sick per worker per year**
Oyez Engineering	6
Breakers Inc.	9
Iron & Steel to order	5
Daniel's Motor Co.	3
National average	5

a. Which firms have higher than average absenteeism?

b. Which firm probably has the lowest levels of stress?

c. Which firm probably has the lowest levels of job satisfaction?

d. Which firm probably has the highest levels of stress?

e. Which firm probably values its employees the most?

Exercise 3

Read the paragraph and use a word or phrase from the text to complete the sentences.

Friday used to be the most common day for employees to call in sick. Nowadays, though, sick leave is at its highest on Monday, with 55% of all time off through ill health occurring then. Fridays are now more attractive, with casual dress codes and early finishes, and employees are more motivated to work at the end of the week.

1. The most common day for people to ________________ is the first day of the week.

2. Previously, ________________ peaked on the last day of the week.

3. Because companies have introduced ________________ and allow employees to finish work early, they like working on a Friday.

4. Productivity is now at its lowest on ________________s.

Reflection

How many days' leave do people usually get in your country?
How does that compare with other countries?

Module 3 The money side

Good financial management is essential for the success of a company. Regardless of how successful or good the product or service, if cash flow is not managed properly and costs are not kept under control, then the company will fail.

Topic 9 Business performance

9.1 Boom and bust
9.2 Stocks and shares
9.3 Describing trading performance
9.4 Market trends
9.5 When things go wrong

Topic 10 Increasing sales

10.1 Making a profit
10.2 Growth and expansion
10.3 Pricing
10.4 Relocating the business
10.5 Repositioning the brand

Topic 11 Finance

11.1 Payment and credit
11.2 Costs
11.3 Accounting
11.4 Owing money
11.5 Financing expansion

TOPIC 9.1 Boom and bust

A boom-bust cycle is a rapid increase in business activity in the economy, followed by a rapid decrease in business activity.

See also

Topic 14.2 **recession**

stock-market collapse

(stock-market collapses)

N-COUNT

A **stock-market collapse** is a sudden decrease in value among all the shares on a particular country's stock market, for example because of a political crisis.

With the stock-market collapse and people out of work, the probability of civil disorder was very high.

You can also talk about a **stock-market crash**.

N-COUNT

If a particular company suffers a **stock-market collapse**, its shares suddenly decrease to a very low value.

They claim that media reports led to the company's stock-market collapse.

go bust

PHRASE

If a company **goes bust**, it loses so much money that it is forced to close down.

The company went bust last May.

bull market

(bull markets)

N-COUNT

A **bull market** is a situation on the stock market when people are buying a lot of shares because they expect that the shares will increase in value and that they will be able to make a profit by selling them again after a short time.

Interest rates quite often rise in the early stages of a bull market.

boom

(booms)

N-COUNT

If there is a **boom** in the economy, there is a sudden large increase in economic activity, for example in the amount of things that are being bought and sold.

When the economy was at the height of the dotcom boom, remuneration packages included flash cars and other perks.

If a market is **booming**, the amount of things being bought or sold in that market is increasing.

boom

N-COUNT

COLLOCATIONS

a consumer / an economic / a market / the dotcom / the housing — **boom**

bear market

(bear markets)

N-COUNT

A **bear market** is a situation on the stock market when people are selling a lot of shares because they expect that the shares will decrease in value and that they will be able to make a profit by buying them again after a short time.

Bear markets usually begin when share prices are high in relation to earnings.

bubble

(bubbles)

N-COUNT

A **bubble** is a situation in which a lot of people try to buy shares in a company which is not financially successful, or which is so new that no one knows how successful it will be. As a result, people pay more for the shares than they are worth. When people realise that the shares are not worth what they paid for them, they often try to sell them at a lower price. When this happens, people say that the **bubble** has burst.

Even after the collapse of the dotcom bubble in the 1990s, a consensus prevailed that the future of business lay in the 'knowledge economy'.

slump

(slumps)

N-COUNT

If there is a **slump** in the economy, economic activity falls suddenly and by a large amount.

The firm made employees redundant due to the effect of the property market slump on its business.

TASKS

Exercise 1

Put these four words into two pairs – one pair that means prices are rising, and one pair that means prices are falling.

boom	*bust*	*bear*	*bull*

1. prices rising: ________________ ________________

2. prices falling: ________________ ________________

Exercise 2

Use the terms in the box to complete the paragraph.

boom-bust	*stock-market collapse*	*boom*	*slump*	*booming*

An economic **(a)**____________________ is a period of increased demand and production. The period of booming economic growth inevitably peaks, following which there is a **(b)**____________________, or a downturn in the economy. This pattern is known as the business cycle, and an extreme example of this cycle is called the **(c)**____________________ cycle. A **(d)**____________________ market is good for shareholders, but when the economy slumps it can be accompanied by a **(e)**____________________, when the value of shares on the exchange falls significantly.

Exercise 3

Read these headlines from the business press and answer the questions.

a. **City analysts describe emerging markets as 'bubble' economies** — Are these emerging markets a good long term investment?

b. **We are on the edge of a bear market in technology shares** — Will technology shares be sold or bought in increased numbers?

c. **Economic boom set to run for years** — Will demand in the economy increase or decrease?

d. **New market about to go bust** — Will output increase or decrease?

e. **Bull market set to last all year** — If you buy shares today and sell in a few months' time, will you make money?

Mini Webquest

- Find out about the **dotcom bubble** of the late 1990s.

TOPIC 9.2 Stocks and shares

A company's shares are the many equal parts into which its ownership is divided. Stock certificates can be bought by people as an investment.

shareholder
(shareholders)

N-COUNT

A **shareholder** is a person who owns shares in a company.

Each of the four shareholders now has 25%.

bond
(bonds)

N-COUNT

When a government or company issues a **bond**, it borrows money from investors. The certificate which is issued to investors who lend money is also called a **bond**.

Most of it will be financed by government bonds.

dividend
(dividends)

N-COUNT

A **dividend** is the part of a company's profits which is paid to people who have shares in the company.

The first quarter dividend has been increased by nearly 4%.

yield
(yields, yielding, yielded)

VERB

If a tax or investment **yields** an amount of money or profit, this money or profit is obtained from it.

It yielded a profit of at least $36 million.

N-COUNT

The **yield** on a tax or investment is the amount of money or profit that it makes.

Today, with an annual dividend of $2, the yield on your initial investment is now 13 per cent.

share price
(share prices)

N-COUNT

The **share price** is the price at which a company's shares are bought and sold.

The impact is reflected in the company's share price, which has slumped to £10.13.

stock exchange
(stock exchanges)

N-COUNT

A **stock exchange** is a place where people buy and sell stocks and shares. The **stock exchange** is also the trading activity that goes on there and the trading organization itself.

The shortage of good stock has kept some investors away from the stock exchange.

stock market
(stock markets)

N-COUNT

The **stock market** consists of the general activity of buying stocks and shares, and the people and institutions that organize it.

Stock markets could suffer if interest rates rise.

invest
(invests, investing, invested)

VERB

If you **invest** in something, or if you **invest** a sum of money, you use your money in a way that you hope will increase its value, for example by paying it into a bank, or buying shares or property.

They intend to invest directly in shares.

investor
(investors)

N-COUNT

An **investor** is a person or an organization that buys stocks or shares, or pays money into a bank in order to receive a profit.

The main investor in the project is a French bank.

investment
(investments)

N-VAR

Investment is the act of investing money. An **investment** is an amount of money that you invest, or the thing that you invest it in.

All income and gains from the investments of the funds are tax-exempt.

TASKS

Exercise 1

Look at the list of shares and answer the questions.

The three columns tell you:

1. the market price of the shares in UK sterling (100 pence = £1.00)
2. the percentage change in price over a 7-day period (a minus sign indicates a fall in price)
3. the percentage yield, or the dividend investors can expect to receive.

Company	1 Price/pence	2 Change %	3 Yield %
A	204.50	2.3	9.0
B	1339.00	1.4	2.9
C	180.50	-0.9	0.0
D	122.15	1.5	1.6
E	366.25	-1.6	2.6
F	374.83	-1.4	N/A
G	180.00	-3.4	4.4

a. Which shares are the most expensive?
b. Which shares are the cheapest?
c. Which shares have performed best over the last seven days?
d. Which shares have performed worst over the last seven days?
e. Which shares offer the highest yield?
f. Which shares offer the lowest yield?

Exercise 2

Use the information in the table above to write sentences about the seven companies listed there. One has been done as an example.

1. At close of business on the stock market, the price for Company D's shares was £1.22. This was an increase of 1.5%. Investors can expect to receive a yield of 1.6%.
2. ______
3. ______
4. ______
5. ______
6. ______
7. ______

Exercise 3

Use the terms in the box to complete the sentences.

investment	*invest*	*stock exchange*	*bond (x 2)*	*investor*

a. The shares of public limited companies are tradeable on a ______.
b. Shareholders ______ their money in the stock market in the hope that their ______ will pay a good dividend, or, in other words, that they will make a good profit.
c. When a company borrows money from its investors, it issues the investor a ______.
d. This ______ runs for several years, and the company is obliged to pay back the money at the end of that period. During this period investors earn interest on the amount of money that they have lent the company.
e. It can happen that a company is unable to pay back the money to an ______, and when this happens the company is defaulting on its bonds.

Mini Webquest

- Find out about the technical difference between stocks and shares.
- Find out about the different kinds of shares available.

TOPIC

9.3

Describing trading performance

Financial managers in companies are now able to monitor trading performance on a daily basis with business management software, whereas in the past they would have received monthly or even quarterly financial reports.

See also
Topic 13.3 **ERP**

increase
(increases, increasing, increased)

VERB

If something **increases** or if you **increase** it, it becomes greater in number, level or amount.

The company has increased the price of its cars.

N-COUNT

If there is an **increase** in the number, level or amount of something, it becomes greater.

There is no reason to anticipate an increase in consumer spending.

level off
(levels off, levelling off, levelled off)

PHRASAL VERB

If a changing number or amount **levels off**, it stops increasing or decreasing at such a fast speed.

There are predictions that prices will level off in the new year.

fall
(falls, falling, fell, fallen)

VERB

If something **falls**, it decreases in amount, value or strength.

The value of shares fell fast.

N-COUNT

If there is a **fall** in something, it decreases in amount, value or strength.

There was a sharp fall in the value of the euro.

peak
(peaks, peaking, peaked)

VERB

When something **peaks**, it reaches its highest value or its highest level.

Unemployment peaked at 10.8 per cent that year.

N-COUNT

The **peak** of a process or an activity is the point at which it is at its strongest, most successful or most fully developed.

He bought the shares when prices were at their peak.

increase / decrease

N-COUNT

COLLOCATIONS

a marked / a dramatic / a significant — **increase/ decrease**

constant

ADJ

If an amount or level is **constant**, it stays the same over a particular period of time.

Earnings have remained constant despite the strength of sterling.

decrease
(decreases, decreasing, decreased)

VERB

If something **decreases** or if you **decrease** it, it becomes less in quantity, size or intensity.

The number of independent firms decreased from 198 to 96.

N-COUNT

A **decrease** in the quantity, size or intensity of something is a reduction in it.

The company said it had seen a 3.7 per cent decrease in sales from the prior year.

improve
(improves, improving, improved)

VERB

If something **improves** or if you **improve** it, it gets better.

The company's turnover declined but profitability substantially improved.

stabilize
(stabilizes, stabilizing, stabilized)

VERB

If something **stabilizes** or **is stabilized**, it becomes stable.

Officials hope the move will stabilize exchange rates.

drop
(drops, dropping, dropped)

VERB

If a level or amount **drops** or if someone or something **drops** it, it quickly becomes less.

The bank's share price dropped sharply.

N-COUNT

If there is a **drop** in the level or amount of something, it decreases quickly.

The company reported a 62 per cent drop in profit in the first half of 2011.

TASKS

Exercise 1

Put each of the verbs showing change into the correct place in the table.

to increase	*to decrease*	*to improve*	*to fall*	*to drop*
to level off	*to stabilize*	*to reach a peak*	*to peak*	*to remain constant*

↑	→	↓

Exercise 2

The eight graphs describe the trading performance of Manton Inc. Choose one of the terms in the box to describe each graph.

grew rapidly	fell slightly	increased sharply	levelled off	remained constant
peaked dramatically	increased gradually	improved steadily		

1. Turnover

2. Costs

3. Sales

4. Output

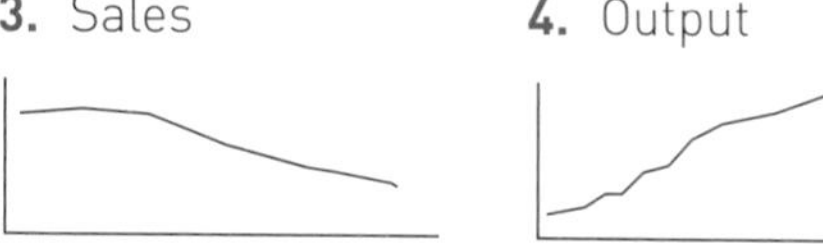

5. Prices

6. Profits

7. Overheads

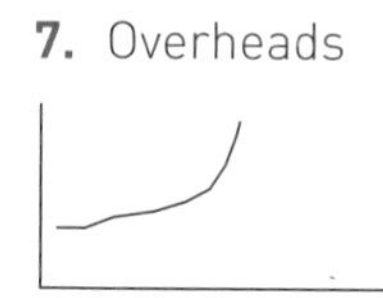

8. Demand

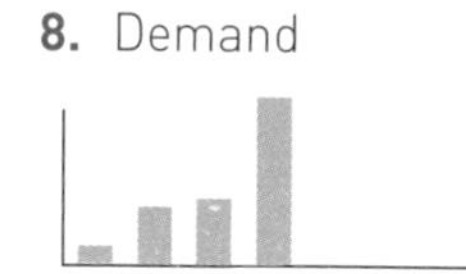

Exercise 3

Look at the bar chart and circle the correct word in each sentence to describe it.

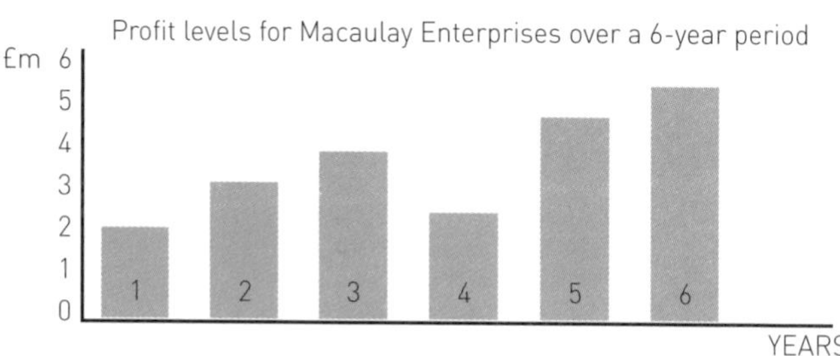

1. Profit has increased/remained constant/decreased over the 6-year period.

2. There was a levelling off/temporary fall/peak in profits in year 4.

3. Profit over the period has increased steadily/slightly.

Mini Webquest

- Look at the share performance of a company that interests you and describe what has happened to it over the last 12 months.

TOPIC 9.4 Market trends

Market trends is a term used to describe the performance of a company, market sector or the economy as a whole.

power ahead

(powers ahead, powering ahead, powered ahead)

PHRASAL VERB

If an economy or company **powers ahead**, it becomes stronger and more successful.

The most widely held view is that the market will continue to power ahead.

You can also use **steam ahead**.

Dubai development is steaming ahead despite the gloomy economic outlook.

soar

(soars, soaring, soared)

VERB

If the amount, value, level or volume of something **soars**, it increases or rises quickly and by a large amount.

Shares soared on the stock exchange.

You can also use **rocket**.

Wheat prices have rocketed world-wide.

rally

(rallies, rallying, rallied)

VERB

When the market **rallies**, it begins to recover or improve after having been weak.

Markets began to rally worldwide.

N-COUNT

If there is a **rally** in the price of shares, it begins to improve after having been weak.

After a brief rally the shares returned to 126p.

upturn

(upturns)

N-COUNT

If there is an **upturn** in the economy or in a company or industry, it improves or becomes more successful.

It typically takes at least a year for an economic upturn to reduce the number of business failures.

upturn

N-COUNT

COLLOCATIONS

an economic / a sharp / a sustained / a strong / a slight / a seasonal — **upturn**

an upturn — in business / in demand

downturn

N-COUNT

COLLOCATIONS

an economic / a sharp / a severe / a global — **downturn**

a downturn — in business / in demand

downturn

(downturns)

N-COUNT

If there is a **downturn** in the economy or in a company or industry, it performs worse or becomes less successful.

The global economic downturn is an opportunity to invest in green tech while costs are lower.

spike

(spikes)

N-COUNT

If there is a **spike** in the price, volume or amount of something, the price, volume or amount of it suddenly increases.

The spike in sales of smaller cars is a result of consumers trading down during tough economic conditions.

recover

(recovers, recovering, recovered)

VERB

When something, for example the economy or a currency **recovers**, it begins to improve after having been weak.

Activity in the housing market is now starting to recover.

You can also use **regain ground**.

However, the pound has recently regained ground.

sink

(sinks, sinking, sank, sunk)

VERB

If something **sinks** to a lower level or standard, it falls sharply to that level or standard.

Pay increases have sunk to around seven per cent.

You can also use **plummet**.

The telco's shares plummeted a staggering 11.62 per cent.

TASKS

Exercise 1

If you were a shareholder in ABC Co., which of these headlines would you like to read in the morning newspaper?

1. **ABC's new management team steam ahead**
2. **ABC's competitors sinking fast**
3. **Following a recent fall, prices for ABC's products are rallying**
4. **Foreign competition power ahead in ABC's markets**
5. **Soaring costs of raw materials for ABC**
6. **Economists predict economic downturn**
7. **ABC's share prices soar**
8. **ABC's share prices are finally recovering**

Exercise 2

Look at the graph and decide whether the four descriptions below are **true** *or* **false***.*

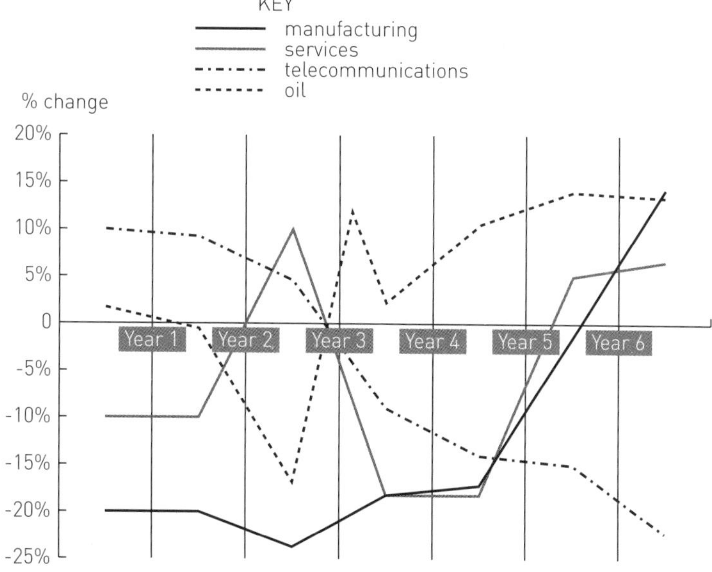

a. After a steady 3-year period, the manufacturing sector has started to power ahead.

b. The service sector suffered a serious downturn 3 years ago, but stocks have soared recently.

c. The telecommunications sector is experiencing an upturn.

d. After a period of steady growth in the oil industry, there was a sudden spike in oil prices.

Exercise 3

Correct the sentences above that give false information.

Reflection

What have been the market trends in your country in the last few months?
What do you expect to happen to the market in the coming months?

TOPIC 9.5 When things go wrong

People or organizations that go bankrupt do not have enough money to pay their debts. They can be forced by law to close down their business and sell their assets so that the money raised can be shared among the creditors.

See also
Topic 7.1 **management consultant**

liquidation
(liquidations)

N-VAR

If a company goes into **liquidation**, it is closed down and all its assets are sold, usually because it is in debt.

The company went into liquidation.

creditor
(creditors)

N-COUNT

Your **creditors** are the people who you owe money to.

They may sell company assets and use the proceeds to pay back creditors.

go out of business
PHRASE

If a company **goes out of business**, it stops trading.

Many tour operators have already gone out of business this year.

turn around
(turns around, turning around, turned around)

PHRASAL VERB

If something such as a business or economy **turns around**, or if someone **turns** it **around**, it becomes successful after being unsuccessful.

Turning the company around won't be easy.

bankruptcy
(bankruptcies)

N-UNCOUNT

Bankruptcy is the state of being bankrupt.

It is the second airline in two months to file for bankruptcy.

N-COUNT

A **bankruptcy** is an instance of an organization or person going bankrupt.

The number of corporate bankruptcies climbed in August.

bankruptcy
N-UNCOUNT

COLLOCATIONS

to file for / to be on the verge of / to be on the brink of / to be facing / to declare — **bankruptcy**

ailing
ADJ

An **ailing** organization is in difficulty and is performing poorly.

The rise in sales is good news for the ailing American economy.

decline
(declines, declining, declined)

VERB

If something **declines**, it decreases in quantity, importance or strength.

Hourly output by workers declined 1.3% in the first quarter.

N-VAR

If there is a **decline** in something, it becomes less in quantity, importance or quality.

The first signs of economic decline became visible.

go under
(goes under, going under, gone under)

PHRASAL VERB

If a business or project **goes under**, it becomes unable to continue in operation or in existence.

If one firm goes under it could provoke a cascade of bankruptcies.

troubleshooting
N-UNCOUNT

Troubleshooting is the activity or process of solving major problems or difficulties that occur in a company.

He built a reputation for financial troubleshooting by repositioning the airline as a low-cost carrier after it came close to bankruptcy in 2001.

TASKS

Exercise 1

Use the terms in the box to complete the paragraph.

troubleshooting	*go out of business*	*turn it around*	*going bankrupt*	*ailing*

Unsuccessful companies may collapse or **(a)**____________________. Companies in financial difficulty are often described as sick or **(b)**____________________. When this is the case, the company may bring in a management consultant to try to help the company, or **(c)**____________________. This kind of **(d)**____________________ or problem-solving is often a final attempt to stop the company **(e)**____________________. If this happens, it will be forced to close down.

Exercise 2

Match each phrase on the left with one on the right that has a similar meaning.

1. The company cannot pay its creditors, and must close down and use its assets to pay them.	**a.** The company is ailing.
2. The company needs someone from the outside to come and give them advice.	**b.** They need a management consultant.
3. The new MD was brought in to try and improve the company's poor trading results.	**c.** It is going into liquidation.
4. Profits are falling.	**d.** She turned the company around in less than six months.
5. The management consultants are looking for ways to improve the company's performance.	**e.** They are doing some troubleshooting.

Exercise 3

Put these four events into the order in which they might occur:

a. The firm goes into decline.	**1.** ________________
b. The firm goes bankrupt.	**2.** ________________
c. The firm requires some troubleshooting.	**3.** ________________
d. The firm cannot be turned around.	**4.** ________________

Exercise 4

Which of the following do you think management consultants would be pleased to find, and which would they be worried about?

	pleased	worried
1. a company facing bankruptcy	☐	☐
2. a company about to go under	☐	☐
3. management trying to turn things around	☐	☐
4. a company threatened with liquidation if its results don't improve	☐	☐
5. an ailing company	☐	☐
6. troubleshooting strategies to improve the situation	☐	☐

Mini Webquest

- Find out about **Chapter 11** of the **US Bankruptcy Code** and what it allows ailing companies to do.

TOPIC 10.1 Making a profit

Making a profit is the core objective of business. Without a profit, shareholders cannot be paid their dividends and money cannot be reinvested in the development of the company.

profit margin

(profit margins)

N-COUNT

A **profit margin** is the difference between the selling price of a product and the cost of producing and marketing it.

The company said profits had also been boosted by sales of vehicles that had better profit margins.

gross

ADJ

Gross means the total amount of something, especially money, before any has been taken away.

The business is already generating 70 per cent gross profit.

ADV

If a sum of money is paid **gross**, it is paid before any money has been subtracted from it.

Interest is paid gross, rather than having tax deducted.

mark-up

(mark-ups)

N-COUNT

A **mark-up** is an increase in the price of something, for example the difference between its cost and the price that it is sold for.

Restaurants make a decision as to what mark-up they require.

profitability

N-UNCOUNT

A company's **profitability** is its ability to make a profit.

Changes were made in operating methods in an effort to increase profitability.

profit

(profits)

N-VAR

A **profit** is an amount of money that you gain when you are paid more for something than it cost you to make, get or do it.

The bottom line in business is making a profit.

return

(returns)

N-COUNT

The **return** on an investment is the profit that you get from it.

Higher returns and higher risk usually go hand in hand.

gross margin

(gross margins)

N-COUNT

A **gross margin** is the difference between the selling price of a product and the cost of producing it, excluding overheads such as electricity, water, rent, etc.

Overall sales rose 11.6 per cent, while gross margins improved 2.7 per cent.

net

ADJ

A **net** amount is one which remains when everything that should be subtracted from it has been subtracted.

Last year we saw a rise in sales and net profit.

ADV

If a sum of money is paid **net**, it is paid after everything that should be subtracted from it has been subtracted.

All bank and building society interest is paid net.

break even

(breaks even, breaking even, broke even, broken even)

PHRASE

When a company or a person running a business **breaks even**, they make enough money from the sale of goods or services to cover the cost of supplying those goods or services, but not enough to make a profit.

The airline hopes to break even next year and return to profit the following year.

TASKS

Exercise 1

Put each of the terms in the box into the correct place in the text.

mark-up	*profit margin*	*breaks even*
profitability	*gross*	

When companies talk about a **(a)**________________ margin, they usually mean the difference between the selling price of goods and their production cost, without taking into account other costs such as marketing and general overheads. The **(b)**________________ is the difference between total costs and sales revenues. Margin is expressed as a percentage of the selling price, or as a percentage of the total cost of goods, in which case it is referred to as the **(c)**________________. Both the profit margin and the mark-up are measures of a business's **(d)**________________. When sales reach a level where revenues match costs, a company **(e)**________________.

Exercise 2

Read the newspaper headlines and answer the questions.

1. **ABC achieves higher profit margins**
2. **ABC announces excellent sales figures, but higher manufacturing costs**
3. **ABC announces its Mexican operation breaks even at last**
4. **ABC's mark-ups are too high**
5. **ABC's annual report details its unprofitable activities**

a. Which story is likely to tell you that the company has increased its revenue this year?

b. Which story is likely to tell you that gross profit has fallen?

c. Which story is likely to tell you about the closure of the company's unsuccessful American subsidiary?

d. Which story is likely to tell you that profits can be expected soon?

e. Which story is likely to tell you that consumers are unhappy with ABC's prices?

Exercise 3

Match the two halves of each sentence.

1. The company said its quarterly	**a.** would be better than expected.
2. The company said gross margins in its fourth quarter	**b.** profit margin.
3. We are using workflow software to get	**c.** net profit had risen by 40%.
4. Digital sales yield a higher	**d.** a better return on our IT investments.

Mini Webquest

- Find out about the level of profitability of a company or a market sector that interests you.

TOPIC 10.2 Growth and expansion

How a company expands will depend on its position in its existing markets and the potential to get into new markets.

maximize
(maximizes, maximizing, maximized)

VERB

If you **maximize** something, you make it as great in amount or importance as you can.

Retailers need to understand online consumer spending habits in order to maximize profits.

expand
(expands, expanding, expanded)

VERB

If a company **expands** something such as its product range, it increases the number of different products that it makes.

The company will expand the range of products it distributes.

new market
(new markets)

N-COUNT

If a company develops a **new market** for its products, it tries to sell its products to a group of people that has not previously bought them.

The Internet offers a huge opportunity to reach new markets.

market share
(market shares)

N-VAR

A company's **market share** in a product is the proportion of the total sales of that product that is produced by that company in relation to other companies.

Nokia said it achieved a slight increase in market share in the region.

growth

N-UNCOUNT

The **growth** of something such as profits, sales or turnover is the increase in it.

The company has restructured its American operations and is now experiencing growth in sales of established products.

The market has shown annual growth of 20 per cent for several years.

new market

N-COUNT

COLLOCATIONS

to open up / to break into / to expand into / to move into / to find / to develop — new markets

maximization

N-UNCOUNT

The **maximization** of something is the act of making it as great in amount or importance as possible.

Profit maximization is seen as one of the major objectives of a business.

turnover
(turnovers)

N-VAR

The **turnover** of a company is the value of the goods or services sold during a particular period of time.

The company had a turnover of £3.8 million.

growth

N-UNCOUNT

COLLOCATIONS

to stimulate / to promote / to boost / to forecast / to expect / to inhibit / to slow — growth

expansion

N-UNCOUNT

The **expansion** of a product range is the act of increasing it.

The company is to speed up the expansion of its Internet home delivery service.

TASKS

Exercise 1

Use the terms in the box to complete the paragraph.

expansion	*new markets*	*maximize profit*
growth in sales turnover	*market share*	

Most companies want to do more than survive, and their prime objective is often to **(a)**________________. This profit maximization benefits the owners or the shareholders of the company, as they receive a better dividend at the end of the year. Companies frequently set themselves other objectives, though, in order to help their business grow. These objectives may include selling into **(b)**________________, **(c)**________________, growth in profits, **(d)**________________ of the product range and increase in **(e)**________________.

Exercise 2

Match the two halves of each sentence.

1. At the moment our firm has 25% of the available sales, but we want to increase this to 30% over the next 5 years;	**a.** in other words, we're expanding the product range.
2. Other businesses seem to have a growth rate of about 5% per year and we want to achieve the same level;	**b.** in other words, we're selling into new markets.
3. We've never sold our software range in Asia before this year;	**c.** in other words, we want to increase our market share.
4. As well as clothes, our company is moving into footwear;	**d.** in other words, we're maximizing profits.
5. We need to sell more products. We're aiming to increase our sales by 10% this year;	**e.** in other words, we're focusing on a growth in profits.
6. Despite the possible long-term disadvantages, we are operating at the level which brings in the most money now;	**f.** in other words, we're trying to increase our sales turnover.

Exercise 3

*Match each of the four sales objectives **1–4** with the correct description.*

1. growth in sales turnover	**a.** Having a wider range of markets should lead to more profit.
2. expansion of the product range	**b.** Selling more should lead to higher turnover.
3. selling into new markets	**c.** Selling more of this product than other companies will increase our share.
4. increasing market share	**d.** Selling a wider variety of products should increase profits.

Exercise 4

*Are the following sentences **true** or **false**?*

	True	False
1. Sales maximization is the same as expansion.	☐	☐
2. If sales increase, then turnover increases.	☐	☐
3. If a company is successful in finding a new market for its products, turnover will increase.	☐	☐

Mini Webquest

- Find out about a company that is expanding into new markets. How are they going about this?

TOPIC 10.3 Pricing

In a very competitive sales environment companies have to come up with sales strategies that will achieve their objectives.

See also
Topic 14.3 **monopoly, rival**

price discrimination

N-UNCOUNT

Price discrimination is the practice of charging different prices to different consumers or in different markets for the same products or services.

Price discrimination can in principle be pro-competitive.

price fixing

N-UNCOUNT

If competing companies practise **price fixing**, they agree to charge the same price as each other for similar products or services.

The supermarket has been fined millions for price fixing by the Office of Fair Trading.

predatory pricing

N-UNCOUNT

If a company practises **predatory pricing**, it charges a much lower price for its products or services than its competitors in order to force them out of the market.

The superstores were engaged in predatory pricing – driving bakeries out of business by selling bread at less than the cost of production.

loss leader

(loss leaders)

N-COUNT

A **loss leader** is an item that is sold at such a low price that it makes a loss, in the hope that customers will be attracted by it and buy other goods at the same shop.

It is impossible for pubs to compete with the cheap alcohol sold as loss leaders by the supermarkets.

price war

(price wars)

N-COUNT

If competing companies are involved in a **price war**, they each try to gain an advantage by lowering their prices as much as possible in order to sell more of their products or services and damage their competitors financially.

Both supermarkets have cut food prices by up to 50 per cent in a move that may spark a price war.

cartel

(cartels)

N-COUNT

A **cartel** is an association of similar companies or businesses that have grouped together in order to prevent competition and to control prices.

He was sacked amid revelations that the company was involved in an illegal price-fixing cartel.

undercut

(undercuts, undercutting, undercut)

VERB

If you **undercut** someone or **undercut** their prices, you sell a product more cheaply than they do.

The firm will be able to undercut its competitors whilst still making a profit.

undercut

VERB

COLLOCATIONS

to undercut
- a competitor
- a rival
- prices

collude

(colludes, colluding, colluded)

VERB

If one person, company or organization **colludes** with another, they co-operate with them illegally or secretly.

They faced allegations that they had colluded with other suppliers to fix the price of bread.

TASKS

Exercise 1

Use the terms in the box to complete the paragraph.

price fixing	*predatory pricing*	*price wars*	*cartel*	*collude*	*undercuts*

When a business sells a product at a lower price than its competitors, it **(a)**________________ them. Companies responding to each others' price cuts by lowering prices further engage in **(b)**________________. Firms which charge lower prices to hurt their rivals or to drive them out of the market practise **(c)**________________. When there are many businesses in a particular market but only a few companies dominate it, many companies follow the price set by the market leader. In extreme cases firms might even **(d)**________________ with other companies, and practise **(e)**________________. This activity is often illegal. A group of suppliers who agree to fix a price for their products are known as a **(f)**________________. Often a cartel will exploit the consumer by overpricing their goods, because they are able to suppress competition.

Exercise 2

Tick (✓) a column to show who benefits first in each case:

	the seller	the consumer
predatory pricing	☐	☐
price wars	☐	☐
price discrimination	☐	☐
cartels	☐	☐
loss leaders	☐	☐

Exercise 3

What are the following examples of? Choose from the terms listed in the exercise above.

1. Company A, a supermarket, buys milk at 115p per litre and sells it at 100p per litre in the hope that customers will buy other more expensive products.
2. Company B manufactures all kinds of household electrical appliances. It has just come into competition with a new company that makes only food mixers. Company X has cut the price of its mixers by 25%.
3. Company C is a bank. It charges its business customers 40p for each cheque they write, but this service is free to individual account holders.
4. Company D has just reduced the price of its newspapers by 5p after its main rival announced that it was reducing its price by 3p.
5. Companies F, G and H have got together to set up an agency to coordinate the marketing of their products.

Exercise 4

Choose the correct term in each sentence.

1. If a government is keen to increase competition it might pass laws against:
   a. undercutting prices **b.** the operation of cartels **c.** price wars
2. Which of the following is likely to lead to higher prices?
   a. selling loss leaders **b.** price fixing **c.** undercutting competitors' prices

Mini Webquest

- Find stories about illegal price fixing and cartels.

TOPIC 10.4

Relocating the business

Companies relocate their factories, headquarters and offices for a variety of reasons, for example to save money or to access a better skills base.

synergy
(synergies)

N-VAR

If there is **synergy** between two or more organizations or groups, they are more successful when they work together than when they work separately.

Clustering allows synergy and support between similar businesses.

cluster
(clusters)

N-COUNT

A **cluster** is a geographical area, usually linked to a university, where there are a lot of private companies, especially ones concerned with high technology.

The San Francisco Bay Area remains the world's largest biotech cluster.

manufacturing base
(manufacturing bases)

N-COUNT

The **manufacturing base** of a country or area is all the factories or companies that produce goods there.

I think it's very important for Connecticut to maintain a manufacturing base.

enterprise zone
(enterprise zones)

N-COUNT

An **enterprise zone** is an area, usually a depressed or inner-city area, where the government offers incentives, for example lower taxes, in order to attract new businesses.

The increased interest in relocating to the enterprise zone can drive up property prices.

relocation

N-VAR

COLLOCATIONS

relocation costs / expenses

(a) forced / (a) proposed relocation

a relocation package / loan

relocation
(relocations)

N-VAR

Relocation is the act of moving a person or business to a different place.

The company says the cost of relocation will be negligible.

relocate

VERB

COLLOCATIONS

to relocate to *somewhere* / from *somewhere* / overseas / abroad / manufacturing / factories / headquarters

greenfield site
(greenfield sites)

N-COUNT

A **greenfield** site is an area of land that has not been built on before.

The Government has ruled out the building of a new airport on a greenfield site.

brownfield site
(brownfield sites)

N-COUNT

A **brownfield site** is an area of land in a town or city where houses or factories have been built in the past, but which is not being used at the present time.

Obviously greenfield sites are cheaper and easier for builders to develop than brownfield sites.

New houses should be built on brownfield sites.

TASKS

Exercise 1

Use the terms in the box to complete the paragraph.

enterprise zones	*clusters*	*synergies*
relocate	*manufacturing base*	

The decision about where to locate the company is an important one as it can affect sales, costs and profitability. Companies may need to move their **(a)**______________ in order to expand, or move to more up-to-date premises in order to modernize. Often businesses choose to **(b)**______________ in order to reduce their costs. Moving to government-assisted development areas, or **(c)**______________, can save money on rent and taxes. Companies with similar concerns, for example in bio-technology, often group together geographically in **(d)**______________. In this way, they can take advantage of the **(e)**______________ created by working alongside companies with similar objectives.

Exercise 2

*Look at the newspaper headlines **1–4** and match each extract **a–d** with the correct headline.*

1. **LargeCorp to relocate to enterprise zone**
2. **SuperCom to relocate to greenfield site**
3. **Office block completed on former brownfield site**
4. **Biotech cluster third largest in Canada**

a. The out-of-town site will allow the company to build a state-of-the-art factory.

b. A new business development area near the city centre is popular.

c. The company will receive generous government subsidies and pay little tax for 5 years.

d. Numerous metropolitan areas are competing for a share of the biotech sector.

Exercise 3

Put these advantages in the appropriate column of the table:

a. cheap **b.** close to similar businesses **c.** close to customers **d.** space to expand

enterprise zone	greenfield site	brownfield site	cluster

Mini Webquest

- Find out about the clusters at Silicon Valley and Silicon Alley in the United States, or Silicon Glen and Silicon Fen in the UK.

TOPIC 10.5 Repositioning the brand

One way to increase sales is to reposition the brand. To reposition a company, product or service means to try to interest more people or different people in it, for example by changing certain things about it or changing the way it is marketed.

rebrand

(rebrands, rebranding, rebranded)

VERB

To **rebrand** a product or organization means to present it to the public in a new way, for example by changing its name or appearance.

We have decided to rebrand our business solutions products.

re-evaluate

(re-evaluates, re-evaluating, re-evaluated)

VERB

If you **re-evaluate** something such as a plan or an idea, you consider it again in order to make a judgement about it, for example about how good or bad it is.

This may force rival search vendors to re-evaluate how they package and price their products.

upmarket

ADJ

Upmarket products or services are expensive, of good quality, and intended to appeal to people in a higher social class.

Upmarket retailers such as Lacoste and Christian Lacroix felt obliged to offer 50 % reductions.

ADV

If a product or service moves **upmarket**, it tries to appeal to people in a high social class.

It has recently moved upmarket to distinguish its products from those offered by the supermarkets.

dilute

(dilutes, diluting, diluted)

VERB

If someone or something **dilutes** a belief, quality or value, they make it weaker and less effective.

Unlike some of its competitors, it uses its name on all its products rather than diluting the brand.

brand

N-COUNT

COLLOCATIONS

to reposition a / to relaunch a / to expand a / to dilute a / an iconic / a well-known / a global — **brand**

flagship brand

(flagship brands)

N-COUNT

The **flagship brand** among a company's products is the one that the company considers most important.

The company's flagship brand has a 6.7 per cent share in the market.

rebranding

N-UNCOUNT

Rebranding is the process of giving a product or an organization a new image, in order to make it more attractive or successful.

The new logo is part of a rebranding exercise.

public image

N-SING

The **public image** of a company, product or person is the perception that the public has of them or of their values.

The suit is the latest damaging blow to the retail chain's public image.

downmarket

ADJ

If you describe a product or service as **downmarket**, you think that it is cheap and is not very good in quality.

We wanted to revitalise what had become a shabby and downmarket chain.

ADV

If you say that a product or service has moved **downmarket**, you mean that it has become less expensive and poorer in quality.

Corporate giants have been forced to move downmarket in the face of the recession.

TASKS

Exercise 1

Read the text and answer the questions.

In 2009 the company's turnover peaked at \$7.1bn, but by 2011 sales had taken a dramatic downturn. At this point the firm considered moving its brand downmarket in an attempt to reposition the brand. They planned to offer the range in supermarkets. Some analysts warned that the strategy to improve sales by appealing to discount shoppers could damage the brand's public image with existing customers.

1. Were the company pleased with sales figures in 2011 or worried by them?
2. What strategy to improve sales did the firm consider in 2011?
3. What effect did they hope this strategy would have?
4. What is the danger of this strategy, according to some business analysts?

Exercise 2

Complete the table by placing these statements in the correct spaces:

a. New target market may not trust the product because of its old image.
b. Sales might increase.
c. The core values of the brand might become diluted.
d. Potential to increase profit per item.

	ADVANTAGE	DISADVANTAGE
Moving the brand upmarket		
Moving the brand downmarket		

Exercise 3

Look at the reasons for rebranding on the left and match each one with the correct explanation on the right.

1. in response to a changing market	**a.** Companies selling the same product in different markets around the world need to re-evaluate the product's success in each market.
2. because of brand globalization	**b.** The company needs to reposition its flagship brand.

Exercise 4

*Are these statements **true** or **false**?*

	True	False
1. Moving a brand upmarket never means putting the price up.	☐	☐
2. One way to find a wider audience for a product is to move downmarket.	☐	☐
3. A company only repositions a brand in order to sell it in a specific market.	☐	☐
4. A company sometimes rebrands a product to change consumers' views of it relative to its competitors.	☐	☐
5. Firms which re-evaluate their public image recognize the importance of a variety of stakeholders to their well-being.	☐	☐
6. A company's flagship brand is any brand in its range that sells well.	☐	☐

Mini Webquest

- Find out about companies that have rebranded themselves in a market sector that is of interest to you, for example insurance, oil or pharmaceuticals. Or find out about how Mulberry repositioned itself in the clothing and accessories market.

TOPIC 11.1 Payment and credit

Getting paid is essential to the survival of a business. Many small and medium-sized businesses have gone under because their clients have not paid their bills on time.

See also	
Topic 9.5	**creditor, go under**
Topic 11.4	**debt**

invoice

(invoices, invoicing, invoiced)

N-COUNT

An **invoice** is a document that lists goods that have been supplied or services that have been carried out, and says how much money you owe for them.

His £700 invoice was settled immediately in cash.

VERB

If you **invoice** someone, you send them a bill for goods or services you have provided them with.

The agency invoices the client who then pays.

cash flow

N-UNCOUNT

The **cash flow** of a firm or business is the movement of money into and out of it.

The company ran into cash flow problems and faced liquidation.

accounts payable

N-PLURAL

A company's **accounts payable** are all the money that it owes to other companies for goods or services received, or a list of these companies and the amounts owed to them.

Accounts payable were understated by approximately $20 million that year.

letter of credit

(letters of credit)

N-COUNT

A **letter of credit** is a letter written by a bank authorizing another bank to pay someone a sum of money. **Letters of credit** are often used by importers and exporters.

The organization has yet to secure any of the required £250,000 that must be deposited by letter of credit to secure the deal.

N-COUNT

A **letter of credit** is a written promise from a bank stating that they will repay bonds to lenders if the borrower is unable to pay them.

The project is being financed through bonds and backed by a letter of credit from Lasalle Bank.

credit

N-UNCOUNT

If a supplier allows a business or customer **credit**, it allows them to pay for goods or services some time after they were supplied.

If we buy goods and services on credit, we owe our suppliers or trade creditors.

Companies will negotiate **credit terms** with their customers. Credit terms of 90 days for example, means that you must pay within 90 days.

Credit control departments within companies manage customer accounts and will set a limit on the amount of credit allowed to customers at any one time.

bill

(bills, billing, billed)

N-COUNT

A **bill** is a written statement of money that you owe for goods or services.

They couldn't afford to pay the bills.

VERB

If you **bill** someone for goods or services that you have provided them with, you give or send them a bill stating how much money they owe you for these goods or services.

Are you going to bill me for this?

credit

N-UNCOUNT

COLLOCATIONS

to buy *something* on – **credit**

a credit –
- card
- rating
- limit
- risk
- crunch
- check
- agency
- issuer

accounts receivable

N-PLURAL

A company's **accounts receivable** are all the money that it is owed by other companies for goods or services that it has supplied, or a list of these companies and the amounts they owe.

The customer's record is updated, the company's accounts receivable ledger is debited and its cash ledger is credited.

TASKS

Exercise 1

Use the terms in the box to complete the paragraph.

cash flow	*accounts payable*	*credit*
accounts receivable	*invoices*	

If a supplier of goods or services allows another company **(a)**__________________, the supplier will not be paid immediately, but after an agreed period. Amounts that a business is waiting to be paid by its customers are **(b)**__________________. Money that a business owes to its suppliers are **(c)**__________________. When a customer orders goods from a supplier, the supplier **(d)**__________________ or bills the customer for these goods. The movement of money into and out of a business, independently of how much it owes and is owed, is the **(e)**__________________.

Exercise 2

Put the heading **money owed to the company** *or* **money the company owes** *into the correct place in the table.*

19 accounts receivable £100,000 of credit given £250.00 letter of credit payable	32 accounts payable 34 invoices to be paid

Exercise 3

What type of information is likely to be on an invoice? Choose from this list:

a. price
b. an itemized list of the products
c. the date when the customer can expect to receive the goods
d. information about the company's other goods/services

Exercise 4

Read the following text and answer the questions.

Here are four tips that could help you get paid promptly:

• Don't just sell and expect to be paid • Get closer to your customer	• Make your credit terms very clear • Issue proper invoices rapidly

1. What will this advice help you to do more promptly?
2. What should you not do?
3. What should you do with your customer?
4. What should you make very clear?
5. What do you need to do rapidly?

Exercise 5

Match the two halves of each sentence.

1. The firm can borrow and repay whenever it wants,	**a.** minimize the funds which a firm has to tie up in debtors, so improving profitability.
2. The purpose of credit control is to	**b.** was our gross cash flow last year.
3. Five million pounds	**c.** so long as it does not exceed the credit limit.

Mini Webquest

- Find out about **credit checks** and **credit rating**.

TOPIC

11.2 Costs

Companies need to control and reduce costs to ensure profitability.

fixed costs

N-PLURAL

Fixed costs are expenses such as maintenance that do not vary with the level of output.

The company's objectives were to keep fixed costs down while training a competent workforce.

Fixed costs = **direct costs**

expenses

N-PLURAL

Expenses are amounts of money that you spend while doing something in the course of your work, which will be paid back to you afterwards.

Can you claim this back on expenses?

economies of scale

N-PLURAL

Economies of scale are the financial advantages that a company gains when it produces large quantities of products.

Car firms are desperate to achieve economies of scale.

unit cost

(unit costs)

N-COUNT

Unit cost is the amount of money that it costs a company to produce one article.

They aim to reduce unit costs through extra sales.

expenditure

(expenditures)

N-VAR

Expenditure is the spending of money on something, or the money that is spent on something.

Levels of business expenditure on R&D in the UK have been rising steadily over recent years.

cost structure

(cost structures)

N-COUNT

An organization's **cost structure** is all its different costs and the way these costs relate to and affect each other.

We have to be competitive in our cost structure, or we would find ourselves at a disadvantage.

costs

N-PLURAL

COLLOCATIONS

to cut / to reduce / to incur / rising – **costs**

costs

N-PLURAL

A company's **costs** are the total amount of money involved in operating the business.

The company admits its costs are still too high.

expenditure

N-VAR

COLLOCATIONS

to increase / to reduce / to cut / to control – **expenditure**

expenditure – on *something*

R&D / advertising / planned / additional – **expenditure**

variable costs

N-PLURAL

Variable costs are expenses such as labour or materials that vary with the level of output.

As a firm reaches full capacity, variable costs may start to increase at a faster rate than output.

Variable costs = **indirect costs**

overheads

N-PLURAL

The **overheads** of a business are its regular and essential expenses, such as salaries, rent, electricity and telephone bills.

We are having to cut our costs to reduce overheads and remain competitive.

profit margin

(profit margins)

N-COUNT

A **profit margin** is the difference between the selling price of a product and the cost of producing and marketing it.

The group had a net profit margin of 30% last year.

TASKS

Exercise 1

Use the terms in the box to complete the paragraph.

cost structures	*fixed costs*	*indirect costs*	*overheads*	*costs*	*direct costs*

A business's **(a)**____________________ are the money that it spends in order to produce goods or services. Businesses of different kinds have different **(b)**____________________ and define, calculate and refer to their costs in different ways. **(c)**____________________ do not vary in relation to output, whereas variable costs do. **(d)**____________________ are directly related to the things produced, e.g. raw materials and wages. **(e)**____________________ may include things like social security charges on top of wages. Overhead costs, or **(f)**____________________, usually cover the non-production costs of running a business, such as telephone bills, and can be extended to cover R & D activities, for example.

Exercise 2

Which of the following refer to the cost of producing goods, and which refer to non-production costs?

1. direct costs **2.** indirect costs **3.** overheads **4.** variable costs

Exercise 3

Which of the above terms refers to costs that change according to the level of output?

Exercise 4

Match each word/phrase on the left with a definition from the right.

1. variable/indirect costs	**a.** costs that are not related directly to production.
2. overheads	**b.** spending by buyers on products and services.
3. fixed costs/direct costs	**c.** the difference between the production cost and the selling price of a commodity
4. expenditure	**d.** costs which do not change when the level of production changes.
5. economies of scale	**e.** costs which change with changes in the level of production
6. profit margin	**f.** savings made by the fact that costs reduce as production increases

Exercise 5

Look at FD&E Ltd's planned expenditure for the year and answer the questions.

FD&E Ltd Annual Cost Breakdown	£
Factory heating	15,000
Insurance	50,000
Equipment	12,000
Wages/labour costs	500,000

FD&E Ltd Annual Cost Breakdown	£
Rent of premises	50,000
Raw materials	400,000
Staff canteen	10,000
Miscellaneous expenses	13,000

How much does the company expect to spend on each of the following:

1. Direct/fixed costs? **2.** Indirect/variable costs?

Exercise 6

*Are these statements **true** or **false**?*

	True	False
1. If the production costs fall and the selling price remains the same, the profit margin will increase.	☐	☐
2. If the production costs fall and the selling price increases, the profit margin will increase.	☐	☐
3. If the production costs rise and the selling price remains the same, the profit margin will increase.	☐	☐
4. To achieve economies of scale, it is necessary to increase production.	☐	☐
5. Economies of scale are achieved because unit costs fall as production increases.	☐	☐

Reflection

What do you think are the most important things that a business spends money on?

TOPIC 11.3 Accounting

Accounts are detailed records of all the money that a person or business receives or spends. Companies are required by law to keep and publish accurate accounts.

results

N-PLURAL

A company's **results** are the set of figures, published at regular times, that show whether it has made a profit or a loss.

British Airways announced its best third-quarter results in 12 years yesterday.

audit

(audits, auditing, audited)

VERB

When an accountant **audits** an organization's accounts, he or she examines the accounts officially in order to make sure that they have been done correctly.

They audit our accounts and certify them as being true and fair.

N-COUNT

An **audit** is an official examination of an organization's accounts.

The bank first learned of the problem when it carried out an internal audit.

asset

(assets)

N-COUNT

The **assets** of a company are all the things that it owns.

Advisers will manage a sale of the company's assets to generate cash for paying back creditors.

balance sheet

(balance sheets)

N-COUNT

A **balance sheet** is a written statement of the amount of money and property that a company or person has, including amounts of money that are owed or are owing. **Balance sheet** is also used to refer to the general financial state of a company.

The assets on the balance sheet are the office furniture and our computers.

profit and loss account

(profit and loss accounts)

N-COUNT

A company's **profit and loss account** is a financial record, published at the end of each financial year, that shows whether it has made a profit or a loss. The abbreviation **P&L** is also used.

The profit and loss account should show the true income of a business over a period.

bottom line

(bottom lines)

N-COUNT

The **bottom line** is the total amount of money that a company has made or lost over a particular period of time.

He stressed IT security's direct effect on a company 's bottom line.

interim results

N-PLURAL

A company's results are the set of figures, published at regular times, that show whether it has made a profit or a loss. When the figures are published outside these regular times, they are referred to as **interim results**.

They reported a strong set of interim results, with half-year profits up by 18 per cent.

auditor

(auditors)

N-COUNT

An **auditor** is an accountant who officially examines the accounts of organizations.

The auditor uncovered tens of thousands of dollars in unaccounted expenses.

liability

(liabilities)

N-COUNT

A company's or organization's **liabilities** are the sums of money that it owes.

Thornton said the company's liabilities exceeded its assets by about $22m at the end of last year.

TASKS

Exercise 1

Divide these four words into two pairs of opposites.

profit	*asset*	*liability*	*loss*

Exercise 2

Match each term on the left with the correct definition on the right.

1. audit	**a.** An accounting statement at the end of the financial year of a firm's sales revenue and costs.
2. balance sheet	**b.** The audited financial statement of an organization which systematically records transactions.
3. profit and loss account	**c.** An accounting statement of a firm's assets and liabilities.
4. interim results	**d.** A legally required review of a company's accounts to establish their validity.
5. accounts	**e.** An unaudited progress report issued by a company to keep investors up to date.
6. the bottom line	**f.** The most important part of the accounts telling how much profit the firm has made.

Exercise 3

Put these events in the financial year into the correct order.

1. Company accounts published **2.** Interim report published **3.** Audit

Exercise 4

Read the paragraph and put the terms in the box into the correct place.

interim	*profit and loss account*	*auditors*	*balance sheet*
liabilities	*results*	*assets*	

Public Limited Companies (PLCs) are required by law to publish end-of-year financial statements. This report on the financial performance, or **(a)**____________ of the company must include at least a **(b)**____________ and a **(c)**____________, so that shareholders can assess the performance of the company. **(d)**____________ check the accuracy of the accounts. The balance sheet shows the firm's **(e)**____________ and **(f)**____________, whilst the profit and loss account tells shareholders what kind of return to expect on their investment. Companies often publish half-yearly or **(g)**____________ results, especially if they need to warn shareholders of poor results. If a firm is doing well it can report a strong balance sheet, however.

Mini Webquest

- Find out about **IAS** and **GAAP**.

TOPIC 11.4 Owing money

A company will generally have short-term overdraft and credit facilities with its bank, so that it can manage its cash flow through the financial year. There may be seasonal fluctuations for when they get paid.

See also	
Topic 9.5	**bankruptcy, liquidation**
Topic 11.1	**credit**

loan

(loans, loaning, loaned)

N-COUNT

A **loan** is a sum of money that you borrow.

You are encouraged to take out a loan over a long period, often over five years or more.

VERB

If you **loan** something to someone, you lend it to them.

The firm previously only loaned money to consumers via personal loans.

in/into debt

PHRASE

If you are **in debt** or get **into debt**, you owe money.

The bank will make it easy for you to get into debt.

borrow

(borrows, borrowing, borrowed)

VERB

If you **borrow** money from someone or from a bank, they give it to you and you agree to pay it back at some time in the future.

They can borrow money at a low interest rate of 3.5 % per annum.

overdraft

(overdrafts)

N-COUNT

If you have an **overdraft**, your bank allows you to spend more money than you have in your bank account. When you do this, you are in debt to the bank.

Most banks charge around 15% on authorised overdrafts.

debt

(debts)

N-COUNT

A **debt** is a sum of money that you owe someone.

Three years later, he is still paying off his debts.

N-UNCOUNT

Debt is the state of owing money.

When we value long-term debt, it is important to take default risk into account.

interest rate

(interest rates)

N-COUNT

The **interest rate** is the amount of interest that must be paid on a loan or investment. It is expressed as a percentage of the amount that is borrowed or gained as profit.

They demand high interest rates on their loans.

interest

N-UNCOUNT

Interest is extra money that you receive if you have invested a sum of money. **Interest** is also the extra money that you pay if you have borrowed money or are buying something on credit.

You pay interest on the money borrowed plus a premium for investment.

out of debt

PHRASE

If you are **out of debt** or get **out of debt**, you succeed in paying all the money that you owe.

The proceeds from a home sale may not get you out of debt.

lend

(lends, lending, lent)

VERB

When people or organizations such as banks **lend** you money, they give it to you and you agree to pay it back at a future date, often with an extra amount as interest.

If banks lend recklessly, it is taxpayers who are at financial risk.

TASKS

Exercise 1

Use the terms in the box to complete the paragraph.

loan	*interest*	*interest rates*
debt	*overdraft*	

A business often needs to take out a **(a)**________________ to help manage its cash flow. Banks will usually agree to offer a loan, but the business will have to pay **(b)**________________ on the loan. **(c)**________________ vary from one bank to another. A company will also usually have an **(d)**________________ with its bank, which allows the company to spend more money than it actually has in the bank account. If a business has borrowed money through a loan or overdraft, it is in **(e)**________________ to the bank.

Exercise 2

Ajax 6, a venture capital company, lends money to different start-up companies. Look at the table and answer the questions.

AJAX 6			
Company name	**Amount lent**	**Number of years of loan**	**Interest rate**
Allways Co. Ltd.	£500,000	5	10% pa
Bright Brothers	£100,000	7	15% pa
Chris Ltd.	£250,000	2	10% pa
Delaware Inc.	£300,000	4	20% pa
Eva Co. Ltd.	£600,000	6	10% pa

1. *Which borrower has Ajax 6 lent the most to?*
2. *Which company has borrowed money at the highest interest rate?*
3. *Which company will take longest to pay off the loan?*
4. *How much interest will Allways Co. Ltd. pay to Ajax 6 this year?*
5. *Which company will be out of debt to Ajax 6 first?*

Exercise 3

Which of the following benefit most if interest rates are high, and which benefit most if they are low? Fill in the table below.

a. banks
b. loan companies
c. manufacturing industry
d. consumers
e. people with savings
f. credit card companies

high interest rates	low interest rates

Webquest

- Find out about the cost of borrowing for small companies where you live.

TOPIC 11.5

Financing expansion

The financing for a business venture is the money that is needed for the venture and the way in which this money is provided.

all-cash deal
(all-cash deals)
N-COUNT

An **all-cash deal** is a financial transaction such as a takeover in which the payment is made entirely in money and not, for example, in shares or share options.

The all-cash deal is due to be completed by the end of this month.

rights issue
(rights issues)
N-COUNT

A **rights issue** is when a company offers shares at a reduced price to people who already have shares in the company.

A rights issue is the usual way of raising new money once a company is on the stock market.

share flotation
(share flotations)
N-COUNT

When there is a **share flotation**, shares in a company are made available for people to buy.

The company are looking to make £5m in a share flotation.

As well as a share flotation, you can talk about a **share issue**, a **share offering** or a **public offering**.

equity
N-UNCOUNT

Equity is the money that a company gets from selling the shares it owns.

The company offers investors the opportunity to invest in a diversified portfolio in the UK and overseas equity markets.

raise
(raises, raising, raised)
VERB

If a person or company **raises** money that they need, they manage to get it, for example by selling their property or by borrowing.

There are a number of alternative ways of raising long-term capital.

venture capital
N-UNCOUNT

Venture capital is capital that is invested in projects that have a high risk of failure, but that will bring large profits if they are successful.

By the middle of the 1990s, there were dozens of venture capital firms in Silicon Valley.

working capital
N-UNCOUNT

Working capital is money which is available for use immediately, rather than money which is invested in land or equipment.

The business will need to increase the level of its working capital or else it may face problems with its cash flow.

management buyout
(management buyouts)
N-COUNT

A **management buyout** is the buying of a company by its managers. The abbreviation **MBO** is also used.

Speculation continues about a possible management buyout led by chairman Jeff Whalley.

flotation
(flotations)
N-VAR

The **flotation** of a company is the selling of shares in a company to the public.

After the company's flotation, 80 per cent of staff became shareholders.

liquidity
N-UNCOUNT

A company's **liquidity** is the amount of cash or liquid assets that it has easily available.

The company has been forced to cut trading staff to boost liquidity and lift credit ratings.

takeover
(takeovers)
N-COUNT

A **takeover** is the act of gaining control of a company by buying more of its shares than anyone else.

The property firm agreed to a £900 million takeover by a consortium of investors.

A **takeover bid** is an attempt to do this.

There had been rumours about a possible hostile takeover bid.

TASKS

Exercise 1

Look at these newspaper headlines and decide which of the sentences which follow relates to which headline.

1. **Westland Bank in takeover bid for ABC Group**
2. **Eastern Brothers flotation to go ahead**
3. **Xceed technology hope to raise venture capital**
4. **Takeover may be an all-cash deal worth £1.5 billion**
5. **ThinkBIG.com in rights issue**
6. **Management buyout at Clipper Co.**

a. The firm, which has been in the family for 25 years, will sell shares in order to raise long-term finance.
b. The banks were unwilling to take a risk on their revolutionary new designs.
c. The hostile bid for control will be resisted by the group's board.
d. Existing shareholders will be able to buy the shares at a 15% discount on current prices.
e. Senior executives hope to resist the hostile takeover bid by raising institutional backing to take over the company themselves.
f. The proposed takeover will be paid for in cash, rather than in shares.

Exercise 2

The senior executives of ABC Group hope to resist Westland's hostile takeover bid by financing a management buyout to take over the company themselves. Read the list of ways they could do this and choose a term in the box that means the same as one of the underlined terms.

raise capital	*by arranging a bank loan*	*share issue/flotation*	*participate in a rights issue*

1. They will get financial support from a venture capital company.
2. They will invite existing shareholders to acquire additional shares in the company to raise new capital.
3. They will raise equity from private investors or a public offering on the stock market.
4. They will raise money through debt, from a lender.

Exercise 3

Use the terms in the box to complete the paragraph.

liquidity	*working capital*	*financing*	*takeover*

Most businesses increase in size through internal growth, i.e. they produce more and take on more workers. Businesses also grow in size through external growth, though, such as buying another business in a **(a)**__________________. Sometimes growing the business may be the only way that it can survive. Increasing production can lower unit costs, for example. In order to survive, it is necessary to have enough working capital to pay for day-to-day expenses such as wages or bills. **(b)**__________________ is money used to bridge the gap between the time products are planned, materials are paid for and the goods produced, and the time payment is received for them from customers when they are sold. A firm without sufficient working capital has **(c)**__________________ problems, and needs to find some form of **(d)**__________________.

Mini Webquest

- Find out about a hostile takeover bid in your country.

Module 4 Global business

In today's world, businesses have to operate globally in order to be successful. They have to be able to source and sell beyond their national borders.

Topic 12 Business and businesses

12.1 Types of business
12.2 Running a business
12.3 Industries and sectors
12.4 Corporate structure and legal status
12.5 Business strategy

Topic 13 IT in the workplace

13.1 Computer hardware
13.2 Computer software
13.3 Management information systems
13.4 Networks and storage
13.5 Problems with IT

Topic 14 Global trading

14.1 Free trade
14.2 The role of government
14.3 Competition
14.4 The balance of payments

Topic 15 Trends in business

15.1 Ethical consumerism
15.2 Fair trade
15.3 Corporate social responsibility
15.4 Different ways of working

TOPIC 12.1 Types of business

A business is an organization which produces and sells goods or which provides a service. Business is work relating to the production, buying and selling of goods or services.

big business

N-UNCOUNT

Big business is business which involves very large companies and very large sums of money.

Therapy and counselling have now become big business.

venture

(ventures)

N-COUNT

A business **venture** is a commercial undertaking, such as the launch of a new company, in which there is a risk of loss as well as an opportunity for profit.

They will run commercial ventures taking tourists into space.

small business

(small businesses)

N-COUNT

A **small business** is a business that does not employ many people and earns relatively little money.

He now works from home, running his own small business.

You can also call a small business a **small to medium-sized business**, or **SMB**.

We expect most of our customers to be small to medium-sized businesses.

enterprise

(enterprises)

N-COUNT

An **enterprise** is a company or business, often a small one.

We sell to small and medium-sized enterprises through security resellers.

company

(companies)

N-COUNT

A **company** is a business or organization that makes money by selling goods or services.

The company employs about 600 people world-wide.

You can also call a company a **firm**.

Four accounting firms are merging to form one company.

You can refer to a company or business as a **(going) concern**, usually when you are describing what type of company or business it is.

Immunex is a Seattle biotechnology concern.

corporation

(corporations)

N-COUNT

A **corporation** is a large business or company.

The corporation employs 23,600 people.

corporate

ADJ

Corporate means relating to business corporations or to a particular business corporation, for example corporate affairs, corporate responsibility, corporate mission statement.

Edinburgh has been selected as the corporate headquarters.

start-up

(start-ups)

ADJ

A **start-up** company is a small business that has recently been started by someone.

Like many high-tech start-up companies, Emnico chose to locate in Swindon.

N-COUNT

A **start-up** is a small business that has recently been started by someone.

It provides financial and practical support to small business start-ups.

commerce

N-UNCOUNT

Commerce refers to the activities and procedures involved in buying and selling things.

We tried to diversify revenues by expanding into online commerce.

TASKS

Exercise 1

Use the terms in the box to complete the sentences.

big business	*commerce*	*start-ups*	*small businesses*	*corporations*	*firm*

1. A business, company or ______________ is an organization that sells goods or services.
2. Business is also referred to as ______________.
3. The term ______________ can refer to large business organizations or to any business activity that makes a lot of money.
4. Large companies are referred to as ______________.
5. Small companies are referred to as ______________ or small firms, or sometimes SMBs.
6. Business ______________ are common in the IT and bio-technology areas where recent graduates from universities have ideas for new products and want to set up their own companies to make and sell their ideas.

Exercise 2

Find five words in the list that are synonyms for a business (list A), and one word that is a synonym for business (list B) and add them to the table.

1. company
2. firm
3. enterprise
4. business concern
5. commerce
6. business venture

List A	List B
a business	business

Exercise 3

Circle the correct answer to each question. Use the information in the table to help you.

1. Seaton Industries has a turnover of around £55m. In other words it is a small firm/a corporation.
2. Robbins Inc. employs around 300,000 people. In other words it is a small/medium/large firm.
3. In the UK, firms employing less than 20 staff make up 97% of all businesses. They are small businesses/corporations.

	Number of employees:	**Turnover:**
a small business	50 or fewer	£2.8m or below
a medium firm	between 50 and 250	£11.2m or below
a large firm/corporation	usually over 250	usually more than £11.2m

Mini-webquest

- Find out about ways to finance a business start-up.

Reflection

What kind of company do you work for? A small business or a large international corporation? What kind of company would you like to work for?

TOPIC 12.2 Running a business

All companies need a business plan, especially when setting up or developing a business and needing to borrow money and seek investors.

See also	
Topic 7.4	**stakeholder**
Topic 11.1	**cash flow**

lender
(lenders)

N-COUNT

A **lender** is a person or an institution, for example a bank, that lends money to people.

Most lenders charge borrowers two months' interest if they want to repay their loan early.

venture capitalist
(venture capitalists)

N-COUNT

A **venture capitalist** is someone who makes money by investing in high risk projects.

Venture capitalists rarely give a young company all the money it will need all at once.

breakeven

N-UNCOUNT

If a company achieves or reaches **breakeven**, it makes enough money over a particular period of time in order not to make a loss. Any more money that it makes after this will be profit.

We hope to reach breakeven by the end of this year.

overheads

N-PLURAL

The **overheads** of a business are its regular and essential expenses, such as salaries, rent and bills.

Our overheads are much lower as I do not believe in advertising.

You can also call overheads **running costs**.

Its annual running costs were about £3.8 million.

business plan
(business plans)

N-COUNT

A **business plan** is a detailed plan for setting up or developing a business, especially one that is written in order to borrow money.

It may be hard to convince a venture capitalist that your business plan is sound.

overheads / running costs

N-PLURAL

COLLOCATIONS

to cut / to have high / to have low / to reduce — **overheads**

annual / day-to-day / to cover — **running costs**

budget
(budgets)

N-COUNT

The **budget** for something is the amount of money that an organization decides it wants to spend on a particular project, for example building a new warehouse.

The company has not set a budget for the project.

business angel
(business angels)

N-COUNT

A **business angel** is a person who gives financial support to a commercial venture and receives a share of any profits from it, but who does not expect to be involved in its management.

They started the company with funds from a local business angel.

backer
(backers)

N-COUNT

A **backer** is someone who helps or supports a project, organization or person, often by giving or lending money.

He is courting powerful financial backers from both sides of the Atlantic.

profit forecast
(profit forecasts)

N-COUNT

A **profit forecast** is a statement or set of figures which aims to predict how much money a company will make over a particular period of time in the future.

But analysts warn that the company might fail to meet its current profit forecast.

TASKS

Exercise 1

Which people on the following list are backers? Write them in the box below.

1. lenders **3.** employees **5.** customers **7.** business angels **9.** the community
2. shareholders **4.** bank managers **6.** suppliers **8.** venture capitalists

BACKERS

Exercise 2

Look at these titles of business books. Choose one of the terms from the box to fill the gap in each title.

overheads	*breakeven*	*backers*	*cash flow*	*business plan*	*budget*

1. GETTING ________________ FOR YOUR PROJECT.
   HOW TO FIND INITIAL CAPITAL
2. HOW TO DRAW UP A ________________.
   DOCUMENTS THAT SHOW YOU MEAN BUSINESS
3. ACHIEVING ________________.
   HOW TO START MAKING A PROFIT FASTER
4. CONTROLLING ________________.
   KEEPING A HEALTHY BANK ACCOUNT
5. REDUCE YOUR ________________ NOW!
   CUT COSTS TO BOOST PROFITS
6. BALANCING YOUR ________________.
   HOW TO SPEND WISELY

Exercise 3

Which book do you think would have a chapter called:

a. Checking income and expenditure
b. The profit forecast
c. When sales income and costs are balanced
d. Allocating money and resources
e. Financing a business start-up
f. Keeping control of your running costs

Mini Webquest

- Find advice about writing a business plan.

TOPIC 12.3 Industries and sectors

Businesses involved in making a particular kind of product or providing a particular service are part of an industry. For example, tour operators and airlines are both part of the travel industry. A sector is a specific part of a country's economic activity, for example the banking sector or the IT sector.

primary sector

(primary sectors)

N-COUNT

The **primary sector** is the part of a country's economy that consists of industries which produce raw materials.

The primary sector is based on the extraction of raw materials and natural resources; it includes such industries as agriculture, livestock, mining, fishing and forestry.

private sector

N-SING

The **private sector** is the part of a country's economy which consists of industries and commercial companies that are not owned or controlled by the government.

He entered politics after a successful career in the private sector.

corporate sector

(corporate sectors)

N-COUNT

The **corporate sector** is the part of the private sector which consists of businesses that supply goods and services.

Finding employment in the corporate sector will be easy for a person with your background, especially in the accounts or legal departments of companies.

secondary sector

(secondary sectors)

N-COUNT

The **secondary sector** consists of industries which produce things from raw materials, for example manufacturing and construction.

The secondary sector entails the production of finished goods from raw materials obtained in the primary sector; factory manufacturing is a key example.

You can also call the secondary sector the **industrial sector**.

sector

N-COUNT

COLLOCATIONS

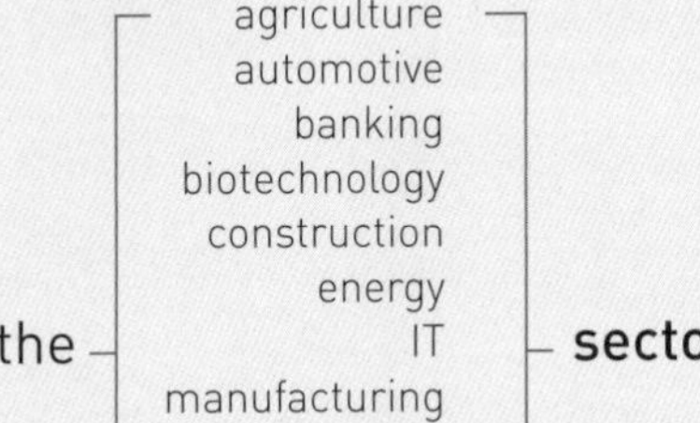

productive sector

(productive sectors)

N-COUNT

The **productive sectors** of a country's economy are the parts consisting of industries and companies which produce goods that can be sold at home or abroad.

The productive sectors of the economy appear to be in recession, with only services showing any sign of life.

tertiary sector

(tertiary sectors)

N-COUNT

The **tertiary sector** consists of industries which provide a service, such as transport and finance.

It will open its tertiary sectors (including retail, information services, consultancy, etc.) to overseas investors.

You can also call the tertiary sector the **service sector**.

public sector

N-SING

The **public sector** is the part of a country's economy which is controlled or supported financially by the government.

Companies across both the private and public sectors still did not view IT security as a core business issue.

You can also call the public sector the **state sector**.

financial sector

(financial sectors)

N-COUNT

The **financial sector** is the part of the private sector which consists of businesses that provide financial services.

Many of them derive their wealth directly from the financial sector, working for hedge funds, private-equity firms or investment banks.

TASKS

Exercise 1

There are many ways of describing the different parts of the economy. Look at the two diagrams showing the main classifications of economic activity and answer the questions.

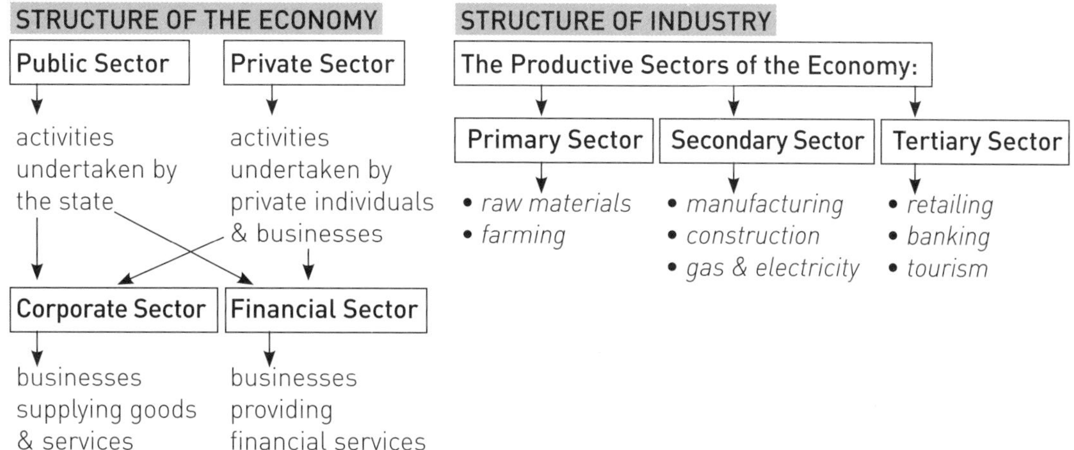

Put each of the following examples of economic activity in the correct column in the table below.

a. Machinery hire
b. Pig farming
c. Catering
d. Insurance
e. Car production
f. Coal mining
g. Oil drilling
h. Graphic design
i. Supply of water
j. Ship building
k. House building
l. Forestry
m. Computer programming
n. Financial services
o. Car hire
p. Food processing
q. Gold mining
r. Producing clothes

the primary sector	**the secondary sector** (*or* the industrial sector)	**the tertiary sector** (*or* the service sector)

Exercise 2

Developed countries have small primary sectors and large secondary and tertiary sectors, whereas developing countries depend mainly on the primary sector. Look at this table and answer the questions that follow it.

Country	**Primary Sector as % of total economy**	**Secondary Sector as % of total economy**	**Tertiary Sector as % of total economy**
A	10%	35%	55%
B	65%	20%	15%
C	30%	50%	20%

Which country do you think is likely to be described as:

1. an underdeveloped economy **2.** a developing economy **3.** a developed economy

Exercise 3

Complete the sentences with an appropriate term from the box.

industries	*public*	*private*	*financial*	*productive*	*service*

a. The manufacturing sector consists of a variety of manufacturing ______.
b. Companies that are owned by shareholders or private individuals are in the ______ sector.
c. A nationalized industry, run by the state, is in the ______ sector.
d. Any company that produces goods or products is in the ______ sector.
e. Banks are located within the ______ sector of the economy, or in the ______ sector of industry.

Reflection

What are the main industry sectors in your country or region?

TOPIC 12.4 Corporate structure and legal status

How a company is legally constituted will depend on its size and the laws of the country in which it is operating.

sole trader

(sole traders)

N-COUNT

A **sole trader** is a person who owns their own business and does not have a partner or any shareholders.

Sole traders are least likely to default on debts.

sister company

(sister companies)

N-COUNT

Sister companies are two or more companies which are owned by the same parent organization.

Their sister company is also doing well in this market.

franchise

(franchises, franchising, franchised)

N-COUNT

A **franchise** is an authority that is sold to someone by an organization, allowing them to sell its goods or services or to take part in an activity which the organization controls.

There are now more fast-food franchises along the highway than towns.

VERB

If a company **franchises** its business, it sells franchises to other companies, allowing them to sell its goods or services.

The Canadian stores are currently all franchised.

plc

(plcs)

N-COUNT

In Britain a **plc** is a company whose shares can be bought by the public. **Plc** is usually used after the name of a company and is an abbreviation for 'public limited company'.

He wants the society to convert to plc status and distribute shares.

holding company

(holding companies)

N-COUNT

A **holding company** is a company that has enough shares in one or more other companies to be able to control the other companies.

Where the holding company owns more than 50% of the shares of a subsidiary company then it is able to control that company.

group

(groups)

N-COUNT

A **group** is a number of separate commercial or industrial firms which all have the same owner.

Those three businesses add up to only 8 per cent of his group's turnover.

limited company

(limited companies)

N-COUNT

A **limited company** is a company whose owners are legally responsible for only a part of any money that it may owe if it goes bankrupt. [mainly BRIT]

You could also consider forming a limited company.

A limited company can also be called a **limited liability company**.

The word **Limited** or the abbreviation '**Ltd**' is used in the name of a company to show that it is a limited company. In American English, use **Incorporated**, or the abbreviation '**Inc.**'.

associated company

(associated companies)

N-COUNT

An **associated company** is a company in which between 20% and 50% of the shares are owned by another company or group.

Our associated companies may contact you to offer their products and services.

subsidiary

(subsidiaries)

N-COUNT

A **subsidiary** is a company which is part of a larger and more important organization.

The company is now a fully-owned subsidiary of the Japanese company.

This larger organization is known as the **parent company**.

A **wholly-owned subsidiary** is a company whose shares are all owned by another company.

TASKS

Exercise 1

Which terms refer to organizations that control another company, and which refer to companies whose shares are held by another company?

1. a holding company
2. an associated company
3. a parent company
4. a subsidiary (company)

Exercise 2

Look at the four diagrams showing corporate relationships and complete each sentence with one of the terms below.

sister companies	*group*	*associated companies*	*holding company*

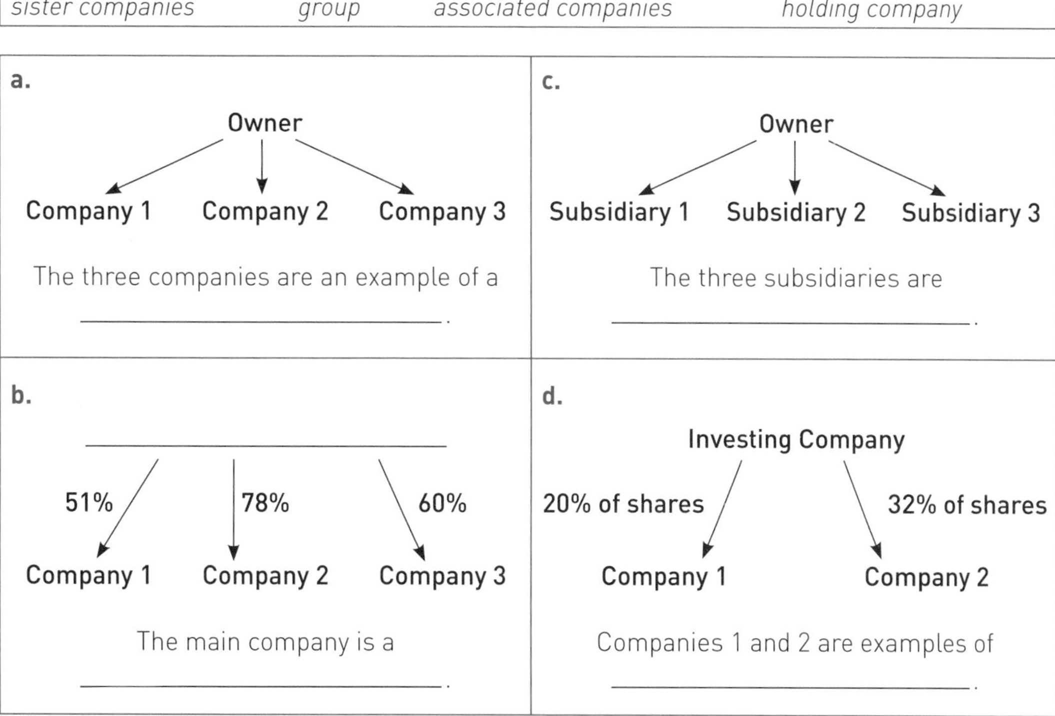

Exercise 3

Read the information about the four companies below and say which matches each of the terms in the box.

a franchise	*a limited company*	*a sole trader*	*a plc*

a. Mike Cobb set up an art gallery last year. He owns the gallery and manages it by himself.

b. Craftplay is a medium-sized firm whose shares are available on the stock market.

c. Ovenclean went bankrupt last year, but its shareholders were not made responsible for all the money it owed.

d. Ultramoda is a large international company which sells the right to sell goods using its name to other smaller businesses.

Reflection

How is the company you work for, or one you know well, constituted legally?

TOPIC 12.5 Business strategy

A strategy is a plan or set of plans intended to achieve something, especially over a long period. It can include takeovers and mergers.

See also	
Topic 11.5	**takeover**

local partner
(local partners)

N-COUNT

A company's **local partners** are companies based in foreign countries with whom the company forms a partnership in order to start doing business in that country.

We have no present plans to have local partners.

consortium
(consortia or consortiums)

N-COUNT

A **consortium** is a group of people or firms who have agreed to co-operate with each other.

A consortium of investors purchased the Savoy Group for about £750m.

merge
(merges, merging, merged)

VERB

If one company **merges** with another, or **is merged** with another, they combine to form a single company. You can also say that two companies **merge**, or **are merged**.

The firm wants to merge with an American competitor.

acquisition
(acquisitions)

N-VAR

If a company or business person makes an **acquisition**, they buy another company or part of a company.

It borrowed $8 billion from a consortium of banks to help finance the acquisition.

expansion strategy
(expansion strategies)

N-COUNT

An **expansion strategy** is a set of planned policies and actions intended to make a company bigger or more successful.

The company is pursuing an aggressive worldwide expansion strategy.

grow
(grows, growing, grew, grown)

VERB

If someone **grows** a business, they take actions that will cause it to increase in wealth, size or importance. If a business **grows**, it increases in wealth, size or importance.

As a business grows in size so limited liability becomes necessary.

take over
(takes over, taking over, taken over)

PHRASAL VERB

If you **take over** a company, you get control of it, for example by buying its shares.

The troubled Canadian PC software company is being taken over by a venture capital company based in San Francisco.

A **takeover** is the act of gaining control of a company by buying more of its shares than anyone else.

joint venture
(joint ventures)

N-COUNT

A **joint venture** is a business or project in which two or more companies or individuals have invested, with the intention of working together.

Consortium banks are joint ventures of the larger commercial banks.

join forces
(joins forces, joining forces, joined forces)

PHRASE

If you **join forces** with someone, you work together in order to achieve a common aim.

We do not need to join forces with another company to compete and be competitive.

merger
(mergers)

N-COUNT

A **merger** is the joining together of two separate companies or organizations so that they become one.

Since the news of the proposed merger, both company's shares have fallen.

A merger of two companies usually involves changing the way the companies are organized. This process is called **restructuring**.

TASKS

Exercise 1

Look at the terms in the box and find two terms that refer to:

a. two or more companies working together

b. an increase in the size of the business

c. gaining control of another company

d. coming together formally or informally

acquisition	*expansion*	*join forces*	*consortium*
grow the business	*merge*	*joint venture*	*takeover*

Exercise 2

*Are the following statements **true** or **false**?*

	True	False
1. In a consortium, the companies concerned continue to exist independently of each other.	☐	☐
2. Only one company invests in a joint venture.	☐	☐
3. A merger is intended to be temporary.	☐	☐
4. In a takeover, one of the companies may not like the idea of union.	☐	☐
5. During an acquisition, one company may be taken over by another.	☐	☐
6. Local partners are businesses which are based in a company's local area.	☐	☐
7. If a company joins forces with another company, one company takes control of the other.	☐	☐

Exercise 3

Use the terms in the box to complete the paragraph.

local partner	*business strategy*	*expansion strategy*

A common **(a)**________________ designed to increase market share is selling into new markets. It can be quite difficult to break into an overseas market, and finding a **(b)**________________ can be very helpful. Their knowledge of local conditions makes it easier for the company to establish itself. If a company pursues such an **(c)**________________ aggressively they will eventually have an international presence or global reach.

Exercise 4

Match the business strategies with the situations below.

takeover	*joint venture*	*local partner*

1. Cool-Cola is a British company. They would like to launch their product in Japan, and would like a Japanese company to help them to do this. They need a ________________.

2. Supersavers is an ailing supermarket chain. BigFood plans to buy enough shares to take control of the company. It is planning a ________________.

3. Max and Sarah have put their money together to develop a new computer game for the British market. This is a ________________.

Reflection

What mergers or acquisitions have taken place in your country recently?

Mini Webquest

- Choose an industry sector and find out about the takeovers that have taken place in the last twenty years.

TOPIC 13.1 Computer hardware

Computer hardware comprises the physical components of your computer set-up, for example the monitor.

laptop
(laptops)

N-COUNT

A **laptop** is a small portable computer.

The group also reviewed its desktop computers, laptops and server hardware.

A laptop can also be called a **laptop computer**.

smartphone
(smartphones)

N-COUNT

A **smartphone** is a type of mobile phone that can perform many of the operations that a computer does, such as accessing the Internet.

The company has moved into the portable music player and smartphone markets.

peripheral
(peripherals)

N-COUNT

Peripherals are devices that can be attached to computers.

A network links computers, electronics and peripherals such as printers so that information can be shared among them.

touch-screen
(touch-screens)

N-COUNT

A **touch-screen** is a screen that allows the user to give commands to an electronic device by touching parts of the screen rather than by using keys.

The new handset features a touch-screen.

hardware

N-UNCOUNT

In computer systems, the term **hardware** refers to the machines themselves, as opposed to the programs which tell the machines what to do.

The organisation replaced both hardware and software after a strategic review.

wireless

ADJ

Wireless technology uses radio waves rather than electricity and therefore does not require any wires.

All our latest laptop models have wireless connectivity built in.

wireless

ADJ

COLLOCATIONS

wireless –
- technology
- communication
- connectivity
- access
- device
- network
- Internet

desktop

ADJ

Desktop computers are a convenient size for using on a desk or table, but are not designed to be portable.

The company is upgrading its desktop PCs and software systems.

tablet
(tablets)

N-COUNT

A **tablet** is a small, flat portable computer that you operate by touching the screen.

All teaching staff are issued with a tablet.

A tablet can also be called a **tablet computer**.

built-in

ADJ

Built-in devices or features are included in an electronic device as part of it, rather than being separate.

A built-in microphone will record your commentary.

TASKS

Exercise 1

Use the terms in the box to complete the paragraph.

wireless	*smartphones*	*laptop*	*touch-screens*	*hardware*
tablets	*peripherals*	*built-in*	*desktop*	

Computer **(a)**__________________ refers to the machines or physical components of your computer set-up. A standard office **(b)**__________________ computer set-up includes a keyboard, monitor, mouse and hard drive. A portable or **(c)**__________________ computer has a **(d)**__________________ screen, not a separate monitor and, as an alternative to the mouse, there will be a touch pad to move the on-screen cursor. **(e)**__________________ or accessories are pieces of hardware that can be attached to the computer, for example a keyboard, a camera, headphones or external speakers. Your computer connection may be via a cable or connector, or it may be a **(f)**__________________ connection. **(g)**__________________ and **(h)**__________________, or tablet computers, have **(i)**__________________ which allow business users access to their email and other work documents while they are on the move.

Exercise 2

Complete the table to show which of the following terms are computers and which are peripherals?

external speakers	*laptop*	*camera*	*tablet*	*printer*	*desktop*	*headphones*

COMPUTERS	PERIPHERALS

Exercise 3

Match the nouns on the left with an adjective on the right.

1. computer	**a.** built-in
2. microphone	
3. connectivity	**b.** wireless
4. publishing	
5. technology	**c.** desktop
6. camera	

Reflection

What computer hardware do you use on a regular basis?

TOPIC 13.2

Computer software

Computer software comprises the programs that you run and use on your computer.

install

(installs, installing, installed)

VERB

If you **install** software or a computer program, you transfer it to your computer so that you can use it.

The next necessary precaution is to install antivirus software.

open source

ADJ

Open source material is computer programming code or software that anyone is allowed to use or modify without asking permission from the company that developed it.

Linux is open source software, meaning that the code is freely available to all and often developed by large and disparate communities.

spreadsheet

(spreadsheets)

N-COUNT

A **spreadsheet** is a computer program that is used for displaying and dealing with numbers. **Spreadsheets** are used mainly for financial planning.

With this software I can create spreadsheets and presentations.

upgrade

(upgrades, upgrading, upgraded)

VERB

If you **upgrade** a machine or software, you make or purchase a new version which is improved or more efficient.

Customers upgrading from the previous version can purchase the new version for $64.

software

N-UNCOUNT

Computer programs are referred to as **software**.

We are developing software that small and medium-sized firms can download online.

software

N-UNCOUNT

COLLOCATIONS

open source / anti-virus / file-sharing / computer / enterprise / storage — software

download

(downloads, downloading, downloaded)

VERB

To **download** data means to transfer it to or from a computer along a line such as a telephone line, a radio link or a computer network.

You can download this software from our website and install it onto your PC.

run

(runs, running, ran)

VERB

If you **run** a computer program, you start it and let it continue.

The desktop allows you to run multiple programs at once.

word processing

N-UNCOUNT

Word processing is the work or skill of producing printed documents using a computer.

I use my laptop for word processing and designing presentations.

suite

(suites)

N-COUNT

A **suite** is a set of computer programs or software.

The software includes an office suite with word processing, spreadsheet and presentation software.

application

(applications)

N-COUNT

An **application** is a piece of software designed to carry out a particular task.

The company offers a variety of web-based applications such as word-processing or online spreadsheets.

TASKS

Exercise 1

Use the terms in the box to complete the paragraph.

spreadsheet	*open source*	*upgrade*	*download*	*install*
suite	*word processing*	*software*	*applications*	

Most computer users **(a)**__________________ a **(b)**__________________ of software **(c)**__________________, for example Microsoft Office or Apple iWork, when they get a new computer. However, there are **(d)**__________________ office software suites, which are free and compatible with Microsoft Office. An office suite will usually consist of a **(e)**__________________ package, a **(f)**__________________ application and software for making presentations. Software producers regularly **(g)**__________________ their **(h)**__________________. Users can purchase new versions or **(i)**__________________ updates for their software.

Exercise 2

Match each verb with a word or phrase that has the same meaning.

1. install	**a.** start and allow to continue
2. run	**b.** transfer along a line or link
3. upgrade	**c.** transfer
4. download	**d.** improve

Exercise 3

Match the two halves of the sentences.

1. The program allows you	**a.** you to create presentations online.
2. We make open-source software that	**b.** helps firms manage digital content.
3. They implemented a single integrated suite of	**c.** have up-to-date antivirus software.
4. This web application allows	**d.** to create spreadsheets.
5. The important thing is to	**e.** applications across the business.

Mini Webquest

- **Apps** are small applications that can be loaded onto devices, like mobile phones or computers. Find out about different **apps** that may be of interest to you.

Reflection

What computer software do you use on a regular basis?

TOPIC 13.3

Management information systems

Companies use business management software to support and integrate all the business functions.

See also

Topic 5.3 **synchronize**

implement

(implements, implementing, implemented)

VERB

If you **implement** something such as a plan, you ensure that what has been planned is done.

The company will implement a new mail sorting system for scanning and interpreting mail.

integrate

(integrates, integrating, integrated)

VERB

If you **integrate** one thing with another, or one thing **integrates** with another, the two things become closely linked or form part of a whole idea or system. You can also say that two things **integrate**.

Integrating with systems like SAP and Oracle needs a whole business process rethink.

function

(functions)

N-COUNT

The **function** of something or someone is the useful thing that they do or are intended to do.

The company handles back-office functions, such as human resources and training.

Functions of business management software:

- customer relationship management (CRM) from initial contact to taking orders
- invoicing and payment of sales orders
- sourcing components and materials
- supply chain management
- project management
- resource planning
- production planning
- human resources management
- financial control and management
- payroll management

ERP

N-UNCOUNT

ERP is a system that allows an organization to manage all its resources, information and business areas together, usually using software. **ERP** is an abbreviation for 'enterprise resource planning'.

Without the automated processes that ERP provides, large-scale e-business would be next to impossible.

site licence

(site licences)

N-COUNT

A **site licence** is an official agreement which gives people in an organization permission to use particular software.

The Census Bureau has a site licence for Oracle.

In American English, use **site license**.

user licence

(user licences)

N-COUNT

A **user licence** is an official agreement which gives an individual permission to use particular software.

They are offering the software for a starting price of $27.50 for a single user license.

In American English, use **user license**.

external consultant

(external consultants)

N-COUNT

An **external consultant** is a person from outside an organization who gives expert advice to the organization on a particular subject.

Why don't we bring in an external consultant to advise us?

TASKS

Exercise 1

Use the terms in the box to complete the paragraph.

external consultants	*functions*	*specialist software*	*site and user licences*
ERP	*business management software*		*integrate*

(a)__________ is used to support and **(b)**__________ all the business **(c)**__________, from CRM to payroll management. Integrating these activities can also be called **(d)**__________, or enterprise resource management. Business management software suppliers sell **(e)**__________ to use their products and offer advice. Often **(f)**__________ will advise a company on its business management software needs before implementing a new system. Businesses also use other more **(g)**__________ to do computer aided design (CAD) and web design, and to manage specific business areas like law and healthcare.

Exercise 2

Match each word with another word or phrase that has a similar meaning.

1. implement	**a.** outside expert
2. integrate	**b.** official agreement
3. licence	**c.** join together
4. function	**d.** set up
5. external consultant	**e.** business management
6. ERP	**f.** purpose

Exercise 3

Which of the following could be functions of business management software, and which could be actions carried out by an external consultant?

Business management software	External consultant

1. taking customer orders
2. giving advice on a new payroll system
3. helping to implement a new software system
4. invoicing
5. sourcing materials
6. advising on a company's software needs
7. supply chain management
8. human resource management
9. offering advice on a specialist business area
10. payroll management

Mini Webquest

- Find out what business management software is available on the market.

TOPIC 13.4 Networks and storage

Computer networks allow colleagues to communicate effectively, and to share resources and information efficiently. Data has to be backed up to storage devices to make sure that it is not lost and that it can be shared.

LAN

(LANs)

N-COUNT

A **LAN** is a group of personal computers and associated equipment that are linked by cable, for example in an office building, and that share a communications line. **LAN** is an abbreviation for 'local area network'.

New capabilities in Ethernet switches prompted some IT managers to upgrade their LANs.

WLAN

(WLANs)

N-COUNT

A **WLAN** is a system that links devices, such as personal computers, using radio waves within a small area, for example in an office building or a house. It usually allows devices to link to the Internet. **WLAN** is an abbreviation for 'wireless local area network'.

Up to 300 client devices now connect to the WLAN every day, mostly laptops but an increasing number of tablet PCs, PDAs and other mobile devices.

You can also call WLAN **wireless LAN**.

WAN

(WANs)

N-COUNT

A **WAN** is a system that links several groups of personal computers and associated equipment over a large geographical area. **WAN** is an abbreviation for 'wireless area network'.

WANs have removed the distance limitations associated with traditional Fibre Channel technology.

A WAN may connect several **LANs**, or local area networks.

network

(networks)

N-COUNT

A particular **network** is a system of things that are connected and that operate together. For example, a computer **network** consists of a number of computers that are part of the same system.

The TV taps into the home's wireless network to connect with the home's computers and the Internet.

back up

(backs up, backing up, backed up)

PHRASAL VERB

If you **back up** a computer file, you make a copy of it which you can use if the original file is damaged or lost.

Make a point of backing up your files at regular intervals.

encrypt

(encrypts, encrypting, encrypted)

VERB

If a document or piece of information is **encrypted**, it is written in a special code, so that only certain people can read it.

This wireless security technology is used to encrypt mobile data to build secure messaging systems.

storage

N-UNCOUNT

Storage is the process of storing data in a computer.

We provide online data storage to more than 500,000 customers.

hard drive

(hard drives)

N-COUNT

A computer's **hard drive** is its hard disk, or the part that contains the hard disk.

The applications are run from servers rather than being stored on computer hard drives.

cloud computing

N-UNCOUNT

Cloud computing is the use of computer programs that are stored on the Internet, rather than on a computer.

Cloud computing allows small firms and individuals to outsource computer management rather than doing it themselves.

flash drive

(flash drives)

N-COUNT

A **flash drive** is a small portable disk drive that stores information. You can read and store information when you insert the flash drive into a computer.

The user inserts the key just like a standard USB flash drive.

TASKS

Exercise 1

Use the terms in the box to complete the paragraph.

storage	*cloud computing*	*flash drive*	*encrypting*
backed up	*hard drive*	*LAN*	*networks*

Computer **(a)**____________________ allow us to communicate and share resources and information. We need to protect this information or data securely, so it needs to be **(b)**____________________ on a regular basis, by saving it to a **(c)**____________________ device. In this way, we make sure that the data is not lost and can be shared. Information can be stored on a computer's **(d)**____________________, on a CD or DVD, or on a **(e)**____________________. **(f)**____________________ data is a way of transforming it into special code to keep a company's information safe. A local area network, or **(g)**____________________ may be suitable for a single office where colleagues share resources like the printer and have one access point to the Internet. On the other hand, in **(h)**____________________, data can be stored on the Internet, or remotely, and can therefore be shared within a network of users over a wider geographical area.

Exercise 2

Look at the table and decide which network is most suitable for the companies described below.

Network	Full name	Details
LAN	local area network	with cables, for single office with one access point to the Internet
WLAN	wireless local area network	wireless, so no cables required for connections in a local area
WAN	wide area network	covers a wide geographical area, is for companies that want to link offices in the organization
VPN	virtual private network	with encryption, uses the Internet

1. TK Communications has offices in Beijing and Mumbai and needs to share access to data between offices.
2. Leddard Inc. is on three floors of a large traditional office building, which has extensive cable connections throughout.
3. Alba Enterprises has offices in several countries. Security is important to the company because they handle sensitive data.
4. Greens is a small coffee shop that wants to offer its customers free network access to the Internet.

Exercise 3

Match the two halves of the sentences.

1. Many people also carry flash drives to	**a.** cloud computing services delivered over the Internet.
2. We are developing programs for	**b.** must implement data encryption.
3. All government departments	**c.** duplicate smaller amounts of information.

Reflection

What kind of network do you have in your organization?

TOPIC 13.5 Problems with IT

Problems with IT can range from minor issues like someone not being able to start their computer in the morning to more serious issues, for example the network being down, or someone hacking into the company's records.

down

ADJECTIVE

If a piece of equipment, especially a computer system, is **down**, it is temporarily not working because of a fault.

As a result, calls about the web server being down have dropped to almost nothing.

freeze

(freezes, freezing, froze)

VERB

If a computer screen **freezes**, or if something **freezes** it, the images on it become completely still and the computer stops working.

Lots of times, I'll be online, e-mailing, and the screen will just completely freeze.

phishing

N-UNCOUNT

Phishing is the practice of trying to trick people into giving secret financial information by sending e-mails that look as if they come from a bank. The information is then used to steal people's money, or to steal their identity in order to commit crimes.

Web security threats such as spyware and phishing scams escalate each week.

password

(passwords)

N-COUNT

A **password** is a secret word or phrase that you must know in order to be allowed to use a computer system.

Users must enter a username and password.

help desk

(help desks)

N-COUNT

A company's **help desk** is the department that people call for assistance, especially with computer problems.

On average 24 per cent of help desk calls are related to password resetting.

trojan

(trojans)

N-COUNT

A **trojan** is a computer virus which is inserted into a program or system and is designed to take effect after a particular period of time or a certain number of operations.

More than half of all computer viruses, trojans and spyware is created to steal sensitive information and make money.

virus

(viruses)

N-COUNT

A **virus** is a program that introduces itself into a system, altering or destroying the information stored in the system.

The PC may be infected by a virus or malicious software.

crash

(crashes, crashing, crashed)

VERB

If a computer or a computer program **crashes**, it fails suddenly.

The company admitted that its website crashed on Thursday morning, but it had since fixed the problem.

hack

(hacks, hacking, hacked)

VERB

If someone **hacks** into a computer system, they break into the system, especially in order to get secret information.

It is suspected that someone may have hacked into the computer system.

spyware

N-UNCOUNT

Spyware is computer software that secretly records information about which websites you visit.

Most PCs were infected with some form of spyware.

worm

(worms)

N-COUNT

A **worm** is a computer program that contains a virus which duplicates itself many times in a network.

Malicious software, such as viruses, worms and trojans, caused the biggest losses for UK businesses last year.

TASKS

Exercise 1

Use the terms in the box to complete the paragraph.

freezing	*worms*	*phishing*	*passwords*	*hacking into*
viruses	*help desk*	*spyware*	*crashing*	

Most companies of a reasonable size will have a computer **(a)**________________ that will deal with any problems that non-IT experts have. Typical day-to-day problems that people have are forgetting their **(b)**________________, a program **(c)**________________, or the computer screen or monitor **(d)**________________. More serious problems with IT may involve an external computer user **(e)**________________ a company's records to get information illegally or computer **(f)**________________ that are designed to harm computer systems, for example computer **(g)**________________ that replicate themselves within systems or **(h)**________________ which gathers information illegally about computer users. **(i)**________________ is another serious problem, where e-mails are sent in order to trick people into giving away passwords or other information.

Exercise 2

The IT help desk at a large company received six phone calls asking for help this morning. Complete each statement using a term from the box.

crashed	*phishing*	*password*	*freezing*	*hacked*	*down*	*virus*

1. My computer screen keeps ________________ for long periods of time. How can I fix this?
2. My computer ________________ last night and was ________________ for over an hour. What went wrong?
3. I received an e-mail from my bank this morning, asking for my password. Was this genuine or is it a ________________ scam?
4. I think my PC may have become infected with a ________________. How do I fix this?
5. I have forgotten my ________________. Can you re-set it please?
6. I think someone may have ________________ into my PC. What should I do?

Exercise 3

*Are these statements **true** or **false**?*

	True	False
a. A trojan is a kind of computer virus.	☐	☐
b. Phishing is the use of computer software that secretly records information.	☐	☐
c. Hacking into a computer system means breaking into it.	☐	☐
d. If your computer screen freezes, the images on it become completely still.	☐	☐
e. A help desk is a department in a company that can help you with IT problems.	☐	☐
f. If a website is down, it is working properly.	☐	☐

Mini Webquest

- Find advice about what you should (or should not) do if you receive a phishing e-mail.

Reflection

What kind of computer problems have you had at home or at work?

TOPIC 14.1 Free trade

Free trade is a system which allows certain countries to buy and sell goods from each other without any financial restrictions such as taxes.

See also
Topic 4.4 **exchange rate**

protectionism

N-UNCOUNT

Protectionism is the policy that some countries have of helping their own industries by putting a large tax on imported goods or by restricting imports in some other way.

Free trade, not protectionism, lays the foundation for better jobs and increased prosperity.

export

(exports)

N-COUNT

Exports are goods which are sold to another country and sent there.

Exports plummeted by a record amount last month.

domestic market

(domestic markets)

N-COUNT

A **domestic market** is the market which exists within a particular country.

All three countries have large domestic markets.

tariff

(tariffs)

N-COUNT

A **tariff** is a tax that a government collects on goods coming into a country.

The new President introduced import tariffs on overseas goods.

free trade

N-UNCOUNT

COLLOCATIONS

a free trade – agreement / area / zone

import

N-COUNT

COLLOCATIONS

a ban on / to curb / to restrict / to prohibit – imports

imports – increase / decrease / rise / fall / grow / decline

export

N-COUNT

COLLOCATIONS

to boost / to promote / to increase – exports

exports – increase / decrease / rise / fall

quota

(quotas)

N-COUNT

A **quota** of something is an official limit on the minimum or maximum number of something that is allowed.

We have imposed strict measures, including fishing quotas, to prevent over-fishing.

customs duty

(customs duties)

N-VAR

Customs duties are taxes that people pay for importing and exporting goods.

The government may reduce customs duty on limestone and zinc to enable companies to cut prices.

import

(imports)

N-COUNT

Imports are products or raw materials bought from another country for use in your own country.

A fall in the value of the pound makes imports more expensive for British consumers.

trading relationship

(trading relationships)

N-COUNT

If two countries or businesses have a **trading relationship** with each other, they trade with each other on a regular basis.

A far deeper trading relationship with the US is now in effect.

TASKS

Exercise 1

Use the terms in the box to complete the paragraph.

imports	*customs duties*	*free trade*	*exports*
tariffs	*protectionism*	*quotas*	

A system of **(a)**____________________ allows countries to buy and sell goods from each other without paying taxes. On the other hand, some countries put large taxes on imported goods in order to help their own industries. This is called **(b)**____________________. The use of **(c)**____________________ limits the amount of **(d)**____________________ coming into a country. This may protect a country's industry in the short term, but if its trading partners reply with similar measures, then **(e)**____________________ will suffer. If governments set new **(f)**____________________ or **(g)**____________________, or increase ones that already exist, these taxes will prevent free trade.

Exercise 2

Match each headword on the left with a set of examples on the right.

1. imports	**a.** taxes, tariffs, quotas on imported goods
2. free trade	**b.** wheat, oil, tobacco being brought into the country
3. domestic market	**c.** country A regularly imports goods from country B
4. exports	**d.** no taxes, restrictions or quotas on imports.
5. protectionism	**e.** rice, chocolate, wool being sent abroad
6. trading relationship	**f.** customers in the same country

Exercise 3

Match the two halves of the sentences.

1. The opposite of protectionism is	**a.** dynamic trading relationships with suppliers.
2. Imports from outside the EU pay	**b.** the same customs duties whichever country they are shipped to.
3. The EU imposes trade quotas on the number of	**c.** over their weaker domestic rivals.
4. Firms with domestic market power enjoy several advantages	**d.** Japanese cars which can be imported.
5. Businesses must enter into	**e.** free trade.

Mini Webquest

- Find out about the role and purpose of the **World Trade Organization** (**WTO**).

TOPIC 14.2 The role of government

Regulations are rules made by a government or other authority in order to control the way that something is done or the way that people behave.

deregulate

(deregulates, deregulating, deregulated)

VERB

To **deregulate** something means to remove controls and regulations from it.

They have suggested deregulating the labour market to encourage job creation.

subsidy

(subsidies)

N-COUNT

A **subsidy** is money that is paid by a government in order to help a particular industry.

The EU has reintroduced export subsidies for some dairy products.

austerity

N-UNCOUNT

Austerity is a situation in which people's living standards are reduced because of economic difficulties.

The president instituted austerity measures, including cuts in food subsidies and cooking fuel.

law

(laws)

N-COUNT

A **law** is a government regulation.

Portugal needs more flexible labour laws.

business law

N-UNCOUNT

Business law is a system of government rules relating to the production, buying and selling of goods or services.

He is accusing the company of violating state business law provisions against false advertising and deceptive business practices.

law

N-COUNT

COLLOCATIONS

to change / to amend / to pass / to introduce — a law

law

N-SING

COLLOCATIONS

to break / to uphold / against — the law

dump

(dumps, dumping, dumped)

VERB

If one country **dumps** goods in another country, the first country exports a very large quantity of cheap goods to the second country.

The corn was subsidized or dumped at prices below production costs, harming local producers.

inward investment

N-UNCOUNT

Inward investment is the investment of money in a country by companies from outside that country, which the government of that country tries to encourage.

The event will generate significant inward investment for the local economy.

recession

(recessions)

N-VAR

A **recession** is a period when the economy of a country is doing badly.

The recession has hit the technology industry hard.

flight of capital

N-UNCOUNT

Flight of capital is when people lose confidence in a particular country's economy, and so start to remove their money from that country. This often has the effect of making that country's economic situation worse.

There has been a massive flight of capital from the domestic markets following the turmoil in the global financial markets.

TASKS

Exercise 1

Match the statements on the left with a sentence on the right that has the same meaning.

1. There has been a flight of capital.
2. The government is going to deregulate the industry.
3. The company has been dumping its products.
4. The government is increasing its subsidies to agriculture.
5. There is a recession.
6. Inward investment is increasing.
7. The government has introduced new austerity measures.

a. Profits are falling and unemployment is rising.
b. It will put more money into the sector to protect it from foreign competition.
c. It is going to remove rules that limit the way management can operate.
d. Large amounts of money have been moved out of the country in a short space of time.
e. Cuts are being made to the state provision of welfare.
f. Foreign business is putting more capital into its operations in our country.
g. It has been selling abroad at below the cost of production in order to ruin its competitors.

Exercise 2

*Your company wants to start manufacturing in country X. Which of the following points would make you feel confident (***plus points***) about investing, and which ones would worry you (***minus points***)?*

	plus points	minus points
a. There has been a recent flight of capital from the country.		
b. Many industries have been deregulated.		
c. Many European countries dump their products there.		
d. Government subsidies are available for foreign investors.		
e. The country is in recession.		
f. The country attracts inward investment from the Japanese.		
g. The government is considering new austerity measures.		

Exercise 3

Which of the following statements are **true** *and which are* **false**?

	True	False
1. If an industry dumps its products abroad it can cause problems for the same industry in the receiving country.	☐	☐
2. Most governments like to try to prevent any increase in inward investment.	☐	☐
3. Some governments give subsidies to sectors of the economy which are threatened by overseas competition.	☐	☐
4. Deregulation can increase the range of options for management.	☐	☐
5. A flight of capital is a sign that a government's economic policies are popular with business.	☐	☐
6. During a recession people buy more and sales figures go up.	☐	☐
7. All governments like to take credit for economic booms.	☐	☐

Mini Webquest

- Find out what the WTO does to try to stop **dumping**.
- Find out about **austerity measures** and **fiscal measures**.

TOPIC 14.3 Competition

When one firm or country competes with another, it tries to get people to buy its own goods in preference to those of the other firm or country. A company's competitors are companies who are trying to sell similar goods or services to the same people.

See also	
Topic 10.3	**price war, predatory pricing, cartel**

competitive edge

(competitive edges)

N-COUNT

If a company has a **competitive edge**, it has advantages such as new skills or new technology which make it more likely to attract business than its competitors.

The country risks losing its competitive edge without significant new investments in education, research and development.

monopoly

(monopolies)

N-VAR

If a company, person or state has a **monopoly** on something such as an industry, they have complete control over it, so that it is impossible for others to become involved in it.

The company has a monopoly on gas exports.

N-COUNT

A **monopoly** is a company which is the only one providing a particular product or service.

This is a wholly state-owned monopoly, reportedly the largest of its kind in the world.

monopoly

N-VAR

COLLOCATIONS

(a) near / to break a / (a) virtual / to end a — **monopoly**

market leader

(market leaders)

N-COUNT

A **market leader** is a company that sells more of a particular product or service than most of its competitors do.

They are the market leader in online music sales.

competitor

N-COUNT

COLLOCATIONS

a major / to lose ground to a / to see off a / a direct / a close — **competitor**

target market

(target markets)

N-COUNT

A **target market** is a market in which a company is trying to sell its products or services.

Our primary target market is 20 to 30-year-old women.

competitive advantage

(competitive advantages)

N-VAR

A **competitive advantage** is something that makes one particular company or economy more likely to succeed than others.

Smaller companies typically have fewer competitive advantages and financial resources to weather a market downturn.

key player

(key players)

N-COUNT

Key players in a market are the most successful companies in a particular market sector.

One of the key players in this market is Dairy America (a collective of US dairy companies).

rival

(rivals)

N-COUNT

Your **rival** is a person, business or organization that you are competing against in the same area or for the same things.

The two tech giants are fierce rivals in the corporate technology market.

TASKS

Exercise 1

Complete the paragraph with the correct term from the box.

competitive edge	*compete*	*monopolies*
competitive advantage	*competitors*	*key players*

(a)_______________ are organizations selling products or services in the same market, and they can also be the products or services themselves. Competitors **(b)**_______________ with each other. Commentators talk about the things that give one company or product its **(c)**_______________ or **(d)**_______________ over others. Competitors in a market are players, and the most important ones are **(e)**_______________. Companies without competitors are **(f)**_______________.

Exercise 2

Match the beginning of each sentence on the left with the end of the sentence on the right.

1. In the global market place companies try	**a.** help increase market share.
2. Having a competitive advantage over their rivals can	**b.** to gain a competitive edge.
3. If a company wants to reach its target market,	**c.** to become a market leader.
4. A successful brand can help a company	**d.** it needs to use advertising that appeals to that market.

Exercise 3

Look at the pie chart showing the market share of four car manufacturers and answer the questions.

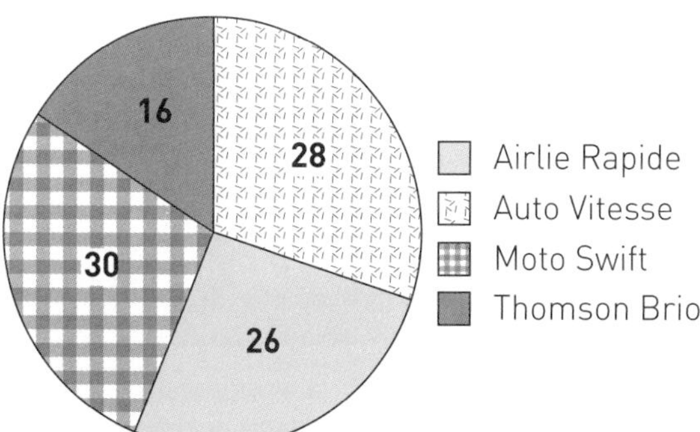

1. Which company is the market leader in this sector?
2. Who are the other key players in the market?
3. Does any company have a monopoly in this market?
4. Which company has seen off its rivals most successfully?
5. Which company needs to develop a stronger competitive edge?

Exercise 4

Read the definitions and decide if they are ***true*** *or* ***false****.*

	True	False
a. A well-established brand name can give a company a competitive edge.	☐	☐
b. If a company's profits are good, they don't need to worry about their competitors.	☐	☐
c. Market leaders often have a competitive advantage.	☐	☐
d. Many public sector enterprises have a monopoly in the market.	☐	☐

Reflection

Who are the main competitors to the company you work for or a company you know well? How would you describe the competitive environment?

TOPIC 14.4 The balance of payments

A country's balance of payments is the difference, over a period of time, between the payments that it makes to other countries for imports and the payments that it receives from other countries for exports.

See also	
Topic 14.1	**import, export**

trade deficit
(trade deficits)

N-COUNT

If a country has a **trade deficit**, the value of the goods and services that it imports is greater than the value of the goods and services that it exports.

The trade deficit has widened and food and fuel price rises have pushed up inflation.

current account
(current accounts)

N-COUNT

A country's **current account** is the difference in value between its exports and imports over a particular period of time.

Russia had a surplus on its current account, not a deficit.

visible import
(visible imports)

N-COUNT

Visible imports are products bought from another country, such as food, raw materials and manufactured goods.

In the UK visible imports have traditionally been greater than visible exports.

visible export
(visible exports)

N-COUNT

Visible exports are products sold to another country, such as food, raw materials and manufactured goods.

Last year our visible exports to Japan fell by 23%.

exchange rate
(exchange rates)

N-COUNT

The **exchange rate** of a country's unit of currency is the amount of another country's currency that you get in exchange for it.

With floating exchange rates, countries can target whatever inflation rate they choose and currencies will adjust.

peg
(pegs, pegging, pegged)

VERB

If a price or amount of something is **pegged** at a particular level, it is fixed at that level. If a currency is **pegged** to another currency or measure, its value is matched to that currency or measure.

Its currency is pegged to the dollar.

trade surplus
(trade surpluses)

N-COUNT

If a country has a **trade surplus**, it exports more than it imports.

China's trade surplus is likely to remain more or less flat this year.

capital account
(capital accounts)

N-COUNT

A country's **capital account** is the part of its balance of payments that is concerned with the movement of capital.

The country's capital account had a surplus of $12.95 billion in the last fiscal.

invisible import
(invisible imports)

N-COUNT

Invisible imports are services bought from another country, such as banking, insurance and tourism.

Imports of services such as insurance, tourism and transport are known as invisible imports.

invisible export
(invisible exports)

N-COUNT

Invisible exports are services sold to another country, such as banking, insurance and tourism.

Tourism is Britain's single biggest invisible export.

TASKS

Exercise 1

Use the terms in the box to complete the paragraph.

visible	*invisible*	*trade surplus*	*balance of payments*	*pegged*
capital account	*exchange rate*	*trade deficit*	*current account*	

The difference between payments made for imports and payments received for exports is known as a country's **(a)**__________. The difference in value between these payments can be referred to as a country's **(b)**__________. The part of a country's balance of payments concerning the movement of capital is known as its **(c)**__________. We can say that a country has a **(d)**__________ when the value of imports is greater than the value of exports. When the value of exports is greater than the value of imports, the country has a **(e)**__________. The payments that a country makes or recieves are affected by the **(f)**__________, or value of different currencies, which changes all the time. Some currencies are **(g)**__________ to other currencies, which makes trade between those countries easier. Goods such as food, raw materials and manufactured goods are known as **(h)**__________ imports or exports. Services such as banking, insurance and tourism are known as **(i)**__________ imports or exports.

Exercise 2

Read the following text about exchange rates. Are the statements which follow ***true*** *or* ***false****?*

If a country has a floating exchange rate, this means that it fluctuates or changes according to the foreign exchange market. If a country has a fixed exchange rate, then this means that the government controls the rate of exchange and that the currency is pegged to other currencies.

	True	False
1. A floating exchange rate is affected by the foreign exchange market.	☐	☐
2. A fixed exchange rate is affected by the foreign exchange market.	☐	☐
3. A fixed exchange rate is controlled by the government.	☐	☐
4. A country with a floating exchange rate has its currency pegged to other currencies.	☐	☐
5. A country with a fixed exchange rate has its currency pegged to other currencies.	☐	☐

Exercise 3

Look at the list of a country's imports. Which are visible and which are invisible?

bananas   oil   cars   insurance   tourism   processed food   rice

Visible	Invisible

Exercise 4

Look at these figures describing the trade between three states and decide whether the statements which follow are ***true*** *or* ***false****.*

ALAND		BELAND	
exports to Beland	£100M	exports to Aland	£75M
imports from Beland	£75M	imports from Aland	£100M
exports to Celand	£150M	exports to Celand	£55M
imports from Celand	£50M	imports from Celand	£75M

	True	False
a. Beland has got a trade deficit with Aland.	☐	☐
b. Celand has got a positive balance of payments with Aland.	☐	☐
c. Celand has got a trade surplus with Beland.	☐	☐
d. Aland has got the best balance of payments figures.	☐	☐
e. Beland has got the worst balance of payments figures.	☐	☐

Mini Webquest

- Find out how your currency has changed in value against a foreign currency, for example the Australian dollar.

TOPIC 15.1 Ethical consumerism

Consumers who choose not to buy products from certain companies for moral reasons, for example because a company harms the environment or uses child labour, are sometimes called ethical consumers.

See also			
Topic 15.2	**Fairtrade mark**	Topic 15.4	**carbon footprint**
Topic 15.3	**environmental impact, sustainable**		

sweatshop
(sweatshops)

N-COUNT

If you describe a small factory as a **sweatshop**, you mean that many people work there in poor conditions for low pay.

The factory was accused of being a child labour sweatshop.

exploitative
ADJ

If you describe something as **exploitative**, you disapprove of it because it treats people unfairly by using their work or ideas for its own advantage, and giving them very little in return.

Exploitative labour can be long hours in factories or other work that is unacceptable for young people.

child labour
N-UNCOUNT

Child labour is the use of children as workers in industry.

The campaign highlights the part of organised crime and child labour in the making of fake goods.

ethical
ADJ

COLLOCATIONS

ethical –
- guidelines
- standards
- principles
- considerations
- credentials
- conduct
- obligation
- dilemma

ethical policy
(ethical policies)

N-COUNT

A company's **ethical policy** is the policy that it adopts on ethical issues such as the use of child labour and matters relating to the environment.

Its ethical policy sets out where it will and will not invest members' money.

business ethics
N-PLURAL

Business ethics are the moral beliefs and rules about right and wrong that are involved in business.

Management must think hard about business ethics and the proper role of corporations in the world.

co-operative
(co-operatives)

N-COUNT

A **co-operative** is a business or organization run by the people who work for it, or owned by the people who use it. These people share its benefits and profits.

The agricultural co-operative has more than 51,000 members in Quebec.

developed
ADJ

If you talk about **developed** countries or the **developed** world, you mean the countries or the parts of the world that are wealthy and have many industries.

Big dietary changes have taken place in developed countries.

developing
ADJ

If you talk about **developing** countries or the **developing** world, you mean the countries or the parts of the world that are poor and have few industries.

Most developing countries are net importers, but some are net exporters.

TASKS

Exercise 1

Look at the list of countries and answer the questions that follow.

1. Bangladesh
2. New Zealand
3. France
4. Singapore
5. Nepal
6. Sudan
7. Ethiopia
8. Japan

a. Which of these countries are examples of developing countries?
b. Which of these countries are examples of developed countries?
c. Which ones are more likely to operate sweatshops?

Exercise 2

Which of the following do ethical businesses or ethical consumers prioritize?

a. values
b. profit
c. wealth
d. beliefs
e. morality
f. greed
g. personal happiness
h. social responsibility

Exercise 3

Which of these four people can be described as ethical consumers?

Maya: I don't buy products that I know have been made by child workers.

Youssef: I choose investment companies that don't do business with firms that harm the environment.

Ethan: We buy the cheapest coffee beans for our café.

Olivia: I invest my money in firms that are likely to make the biggest profits.

Exercise 4

*Are these statements **true** or **false**?*

	True	False
1. Sweatshops are retail outlets selling sports clothing.	☐	☐
2. Sweatshops do not exist only in developing countries.	☐	☐
3. Child labour exists only in developing countries.	☐	☐
4. Sweatshops are exploitative.	☐	☐
5. Ethics are usually the main guiding principle in business.	☐	☐

Reflection

How much do ethical issues influence your buying decisions?

TOPIC 15.2 Fair trade

Fair trade is the practice of buying goods directly from producers in developing countries at a fair price. Fairtrade (or Fairly-traded) products are bought from producers in developing countries at a fair price.

See also	
Topic 15.1	**ethical policy, business ethics**

world market

N-SING

The **world market** for a product is all the people throughout the world who wish to buy that product.

They control 40 per cent of the world market for mobile devices.

cash crop

(cash crops)

N-COUNT

A **cash crop** is a crop that is grown in order to be sold.

Growers are shifting to other more profitable cash crops such as rubber and cassava.

grower

(growers)

N-COUNT

A **grower** is a person who grows large quantities of a particular plant or crop in order to sell them.

Citrus and grape growers say that many irrigators in the region are struggling to survive on low water allocations.

Fairtrade mark

N-SING

In Britain, the **Fairtrade mark** is a sign that is placed on the packaging of products to show that the product has been bought at a fair price, usually from producers in developing countries.

The Fairtrade mark is a registered certification label for products sourced from producers in developing countries.

You can also refer to the **Fairtrade symbol**.

commodity

(commodities)

N-COUNT

A **commodity** is something that is sold for money.

The price of commodities like sugar and cotton has shot up.

per capita

ADJ

The **per capita** amount of something is the total amount of it in a country or area divided by the number of people in that country or area. **Per capita** means 'per person'.

They have the world's largest per capita income.

per capita

ADJ

COLLOCATIONS

per capita spending / consumption

to do *something* on a / to be *something* on a per capita basis

world market prices

N-PLURAL

World market prices are the prices paid for something internationally, ignoring any tariffs or subsidies imposed by particular countries.

This is well below world market prices for natural gas.

producer

(producers)

N-COUNT

A **producer** of a food or material is a company or country that grows or manufactures a large amount of it.

Sidor is the biggest steel producer in the Caribbean and Andean regions.

GDP

(GDPs)

N-VAR

In economics, a country's **GDP** is the total value of goods and services produced within that country in a year, not including its income from investments in other countries. **GDP** is an abbreviation for 'gross domestic product'.

We still have a trade deficit that is 5 per cent of GDP.

TASKS

Exercise 1

Use the terms in the box to complete the paragraph.

fair trade (2)	*world market prices*	*commodities*	*producers and growers*
developing	*Fairtrade mark*	*cash crops*	

The trading company Traidfair describes itself as a social enterprise. It attempts to bring justice to international trade by promoting **(a)**__________________ with **(b)**__________________ countries. Social responsibility is their main priority, and the setting up and maintaining of non-exploitative trading relationships with their suppliers from developing countries, i.e. the **(c)**__________________. Their suppliers produce **(d)**__________________ and Traidfair pay **(e)**__________________ for the crop or the **(f)**__________________ that they purchase, which then carry the **(g)**__________________. Traidfair's customers are loyal to them even though their prices are often higher than those of other similar products. More and more people are coming to view **(h)**__________________ and social responsibility as more important than the pursuit of profit.

Exercise 2

Which of the following are characteristics of the free trade system and which of the Fairtrade system?

a. Producers are often divided by competition.
b. Producers in developing countries have more power.
c. The consumer wants a cheap product.
d. The consumer's main aim is not financial.
e. Companies are motivated by profit.
f. The company's main objective is social responsibility.

Free trade system	Fairtrade system

Exercise 3

Read the text and answer the questions which follow.

Paulo and Pedro live in a developing country. Both are farmers working with about 5 hectares of land. Pedro grows maize, potatoes and fruit, keeps 2 pigs, some chickens, 3 goats and a cow. His family eat most of what they produce but sometimes have a little left over which they sell for cash. Paulo grows coffee on his land. He and his family tend the plants and pick the beans which are sold to buyers from America in the local market.

1. Which of these two farmers is producing a cash crop?
2. Is their country likely to have a high or low GDP?
3. Is their country likely to have a high or low per capita income?
4. Is America's GDP likely to be higher or lower than the GDP of Paulo and Perdro's country?
5. Which farmer would benefit most from fair trade?

Mini Webquest

- Find out about Fairtrade business services.

TOPIC 15.3 Corporate social responsibility

Corporate social responsibility (CSR) is the sense of responsibility that a company has towards things, for example its stakeholders: customers, employees, shareholders and the local and wider community within which it operates.

See also	
Topic 15.1	**ethical policy, business ethics**
Topic 15.4	**carbon footprint**

mission statement
(mission statements)

N-COUNT

A company or organization's **mission statement** is a document which states what it aims to achieve and the kind of service it intends to provide.

A mission statement should say who you are, what you do, what you stand for and why you do it.

social cost
(social costs)

N-COUNT

The **social costs** of a policy or scheme are the undesirable effects that it is likely to have on individuals or on society, such as negative effects on the families of employees, or on the environment.

There will be huge social costs if parents have to return to the workforce and can't put their children first.

non-profit-making
ADJ

A **non-profit-making** organization or charity is not run with the intention of making a profit.

As with any non-profit-making organization, fund-raising was vital to our success.

sustainable
ADJ

You use **sustainable** to describe the use of natural resources when this use is kept at a steady level that is not likely to damage the environment.

The IT community must play its part in ensuring sustainable development.

sustainable
ADJ

COLLOCATIONS

ecologically / environmentally — **sustainable**

sustainable — development / growth / agriculture

environmental impact
(environmental impacts)

N-VAR

The **environmental impact** of a scheme or product is the environmental effect that the scheme or product is likely to have, for example an increase in pollution or a loss of natural habitats.

They have tried to minimise the environmental impact of the project.

social benefit
(social benefits)

N-COUNT

The **social benefits** of a policy or scheme are the desirable effects that it is likely to have on individuals or on society, such as positive effects on the families of employees, or on the environment.

Nations that invest in ICT to transform fields like transport and energy reap substantial long-term economic and social benefits.

social audit
(social audits)

N-COUNT

If a company carries out a **social audit**, it analyses the social costs and social benefits of its operations in order to measure their success.

Their most recent social audit highlighted a disappointing lack of social initiatives at the company and poor morale among employees.

TASKS

Exercise 1

Which of these factors might act to increase corporate social responsibility and which might act as barriers to it?

a. a rise in costs associated with a more responsible approach
b. shareholder pressure to increase profits
c. business secrecy
d. social auditing
e. pressure from society

Exercise 2

Use the terms in the box to complete the paragraph.

social audit	*social costs*	*mission statement*
corporate social responsibility	*social benefits*	

Companies which accept **(a)**________________, or CSR, are prepared to accept responsibility for their actions and are able to justify them. They will consider the **(b)**________________ or the **(c)**________________ that their actions might have on groups and individuals both inside and outside the organization. Many businesses try to assess the impact of their activities on stakeholders, or anyone who has an interest in the company. This process is known as a **(d)**________________, and most companies who carry out this kind of auditing also have a CSR policy or strategy as part of their **(e)**________________.

Exercise 3

Match the two halves of the sentences.

1. Their mission statement is to enable people and businesses throughout the world	**a.** of the oil drilling on a nearby reef.
2. Residents are concerned about the potential environmental impact	**b.** sustainable development and renewable energy.
3. We see green IT as part	**c.** to realise their full potential.
4. He is a passionate advocate of	**d.** of our corporate social responsibility.

Exercise 4

Read the text and answer the questions.

> Oxfam is a non-profit-making organization whose primary objective is to alleviate poverty throughout the world. Most of its funds are used to provide long-term development aid to developing countries.

1. Do you think Oxfam are likely to encourage sustainable development?
2. Do you think Oxfam are likely to include a CSR policy in their mission statement?
3. Do you think Oxfam are likely to support companies which have a negative environmental impact in the developing world?
4. Do you think Oxfam are likely to encourage companies to conduct a social audit of their business?

Reflection

Find out about the CSR policy of a company that interests you.

TOPIC 15.4 Different ways of working

Ways of working have changed because IT allows flexible working and because individuals are looking for ways to reduce the time that they spend commuting, in order to save money and to reduce their carbon footprint.

See also

Topic 15.3 **environmental impact**

commute

(commutes, commuting, commuted)

VERB

If you **commute**, you travel a long distance every day between your home and your place of work.

She commutes to London every day.

N-COUNT

A **commute** is the journey that you make when you commute.

The average Los Angeles commute is over 60 miles a day.

flexible working arrangements

N-PLURAL

Flexible working arrangements are arrangements in which some employees are allowed to vary the hours that they work in order to suit their personal needs.

Employers can agree more flexible working arrangements subject to business requirements.

part-time

ADJ

If someone is a **part-time** worker, or has a **part-time** job, they work for only part of each day or week.

Many businesses are cutting back by employing lower-paid part-time workers.

ADV

If someone works **part-time**, they work for only part of each day or week.

I will continue to work part-time as a consultant after the age of 60.

flexitime

N-UNCOUNT

Flexitime is a system that allows employees to vary the time that they start or finish work, provided that an agreed total number of hours are spent at work. [BRIT]

One in four firms offers flexitime.

commute

VERB

COLLOCATIONS

to commute –
- by car
- by train
- by bike
- daily
- regularly
- from *somewhere*
- to *somewhere*

job sharing

N-UNCOUNT

Job sharing is an arrangement in which two people share the same job by working part-time, for example one person in the mornings and the other in the afternoons.

Flexible working options include job sharing, home working, reduced hours and flexitime.

homeworker

(homeworkers)

N-COUNT

A **homeworker** is a person who works from home using equipment such as a telephone, fax machine and computer to keep in contact.

One in 10 of the company's workforce is now a homeworker.

A homeworker can also be called a **teleworker** or a **telecommuter**.

carbon footprint

(carbon footprints)

N-COUNT

Your **carbon footprint** is a measure of the amount of carbon dioxide released into the atmosphere by your activities over a particular period.

We all need to look for ways to reduce our carbon footprint.

hot-desk

(hot-desks, hot-desking, hot-desked)

VERB

If employees **hot-desk**, they are not assigned particular desks and work at any desk that is available.

Currently about 15% of staff hot-desk - allowing people to work anywhere at any time, with just a mobile and laptop.

TASKS

Exercise 1

Complete the sentences by putting one of these words or phrases in each space.

job sharing	*homeworker*	*part-time*	*flexitime*	*hot-desking*

1. Ben's company demands that he is in the office between 10.00 and 15.00, but he can start earlier than that and finish later than that as long as he works 40 hours per week. He is working ______________.
2. Irfan works for a large insurance firm but he only goes to their office one day a week. For the other four he works at home and keeps in touch by e-mail, fax and phone. For four days a week, he's a ______________.
3. Chloe and Jessica are both receptionists for a PR firm. Chloe works there on Monday and Tuesday, Jessica then takes over for the rest of the week. This style of working is known as ______________.
4. Jack works in a call centre. He doesn't have his own desk in the office, so he has to find any work station available and use the computer and telephone there. He's ______________.
5. Mei works in an office three days a week. She's also studying at university two days a week. She's working ______________.

Exercise 2

Are these statements ***true*** *or* ***false****?*

	True	False
1. Part-time workers do not have a full-time job.	☐	☐
2. Flexitime workers always start their working day at the same time.	☐	☐
3. Companies which offer flexible working patterns give their employees more control over their hours of work.	☐	☐
4. Hot-desking workers have their own desks.	☐	☐
5. Your commute is your journey to work.	☐	☐
6. Working from home reduces your carbon footprint.	☐	☐

Exercise 3

Some estimates suggest that up to one third of the workforce could eventually be teleworkers. List the benefits to a company and to the employee of this way of working. Choose from the list below.

no commuting	*smaller premises*	*flexible working hours*
wider choice of potential employees	*lower overheads*	*no restrictions on where you live*

COMPANY	EMPLOYEE

Reflection

How far do you have to commute to your place of work?

What is your job routine?

Appendices

Answer key

Index

Answer Key

TASKS 1.1

Exercise 1

a. market research **b.** qualitative **c.** interviews **d.** quantitative **e.** questionnaires **f.** primary **g.** focus groups **h.** field **i.** secondary **j.** desk

Exercise 2

1. secondary **2.** secondary **3.** secondary **4.** primary **5.** primary **6.** primary

Exercise 3

1. f **2.** e **3.** d **4.** a **5.** b **6.** c

TASKS 1.2

Exercise 1

a. product-led **b.** product **c.** CAD **d.** reverse engineering **e.** existing product **f.** customize **g.** R & D **h.** market sector

Exercise 2

1. b **2.** d **3.** a **4.** e **5.** c

Exercise 3

1. b **2.** c **3.** d **4.** a

TASKS 1.3

Exercise 1

1. market tests **2.** test market **3.** passed **4.** modified **5.** pilot **6.** fail

Exercise 2

1. S **2.** U **3.** U **4.** S **5.** U

Exercise 3

1. c **2.** d **3.** a **4.** b

TASKS 1.4

Exercise 1

a. invention **b.** patenting **c.** under licence **d.** intellectual property rights **e.** piracy **f.** copyrighted

Exercise 2

1. f **2.** d **3.** a **4.** e **5.** b **6.** c

Exercise 3

1. c **2.** d **3.** a **4.** b

TASKS 2.1

Exercise 1

a. lean production **b.** production process **c.** factory **d.** just-in-time **e.** production

Exercise 2

1. factory **2.** manufacturer **3.** output **4.** output **5.** works

Exercise 3

a. false **b.** true **c.** false **d.** true **e.** true

Exercise 4

a. It will be low. **b.** It will be low. **c.** There will not be much bulk-buying. **d.** Low, because of levels of stock.

TASKS 2.2

Exercise 1

a. futures **b.** raw materials **c.** components **d.** suppliers **e.** tender **f.** sourced **g.** manufacturers **h.** product

Exercise 2

1. Zhang Ltd **2.** A&M **3.** A&M **4.** 2 (UK and China) **5.** Kressler

Exercise 3

1. d **2.** e **3.** c **4.** b **5.** a

TASKS 2.3

Exercise 1

a. total quality management **b.** quality control/ quality assurance; routine checks **c.** quality control/quality assurance **d.** monitor **e.** benchmarking

Exercise 2

1. c **2.** a **3.** b **4.** d

Exercise 3

1, 3, 4, 7

Exercise 4

QC: b, d, g
TQM: a, c, e, f

TASKS 2.4

Exercise 1

a. outsource **b.** production **c.** overseas **d.** third party **e.** firms **f.** core business **g.** increase **h.** subcontracting **i.** quality **j.** relocate

Exercise 2

1. false **2.** false **3.** true **4.** true **5.** false

Exercise 3

1. b **2.** c **3.** a

TASKS 2.5

Exercise 1

a. production line **b.** robots **c.** automation **d.** job satisfaction **e.** job rotation **f.** teams

Exercise 2

blue-collar: 2, 3, 7, 8, 11
white-collar: 1, 4, 5, 6, 9, 10, 12

Exercise 3

1. c **2.** a **3.** d **4.** b

TASKS 3.1

Exercise 1

1. place **2.** price **3.** product **4.** promotion

Exercise 2

1. b **2.** d **3.** c **4.** a

Exercise 3

1. true **2.** false **3.** true

TASKS 3.2

Exercise 1

1. false **2.** true **3.** false **4.** true **5.** true

Exercise 2

a. advertising agency **b.** campaign **c.** advertised **d.** billboards **e.** Internet sites **f.** viral marketing **g.** word of mouth **h.** social media

Exercise 3

1. d **2.** a **3.** c **4.** b

TASKS 3.3

Exercise 1

a. new-pc.com **b.** overseas factory **c.** overseas shipping company **d.** local parcel delivery courier **e.** Bell Ltd

Exercise 2

a. packaging **b.** recyclable **c.** intermediary **d.** wholesaler **e.** Internet **f.** online **g.** list prices

Exercise 3

1. Zedex **2.** Tri-Lite **3.** Sanderson **4.** Tri-Lite **5.** Zedex

TASKS 3.4

Exercise 1

a. brand name **b.** brand awareness **c.** own brand **d.** brand image

Exercise 2

1. brand recognition **2.** own brand **3.** brand loyalty **4.** brand name **5.** brand image **6.** brand awareness **7.** brand stretch

Exercise 3

1. false **2.** true **3.** false **4.** true

TASKS 3.5

Exercise 1

1. true **2.** true **3.** false **4.** false **5.** true

Exercise 2

1. b **2.** d **3.** c **4.** a

Exercise 3

1. penetration pricing **2.** value-based pricing **3.** competition-based pricing **4.** cost-based pricing

Exercise 4

1. opportunities **2.** strengths **3.** threats **4.** weaknesses

TASKS 4.1

Exercise 1

a. good listener **b.** reading **c.** salesperson **d.** knowledgeable **e.** enthusiastic **f.** persuade **g.** close

Exercise 2

1. Y **2.** N **3.** Y **4.** Y **5.** N

Exercise 3

1. false **2.** true **3.** false **4.** true **5.** true **6.** true **7.** false

TASKS 4.2

Exercise 1

a. components **b.** stocks **c.** lead times **d.** orders

Exercise 2

1. logistics **2.** the purchasing department **3.** raw material = metal; component = electric motor **4.** hotels, launderettes

Exercise 3

1. true **2.** false **3.** false **4.** true

TASKS 4.3

Exercise 1

a. distribution **b.** end users **c.** distributor **d.** distribution network **e.** warehouse **f.** agent

Exercise 2

a. manufacturers **b.** wholesaler/agent **c.** wholesaler/agent **d.** warehouse **e.** end users

Exercise 3

1. freight forwarder, forwarding agent, forwarder **2.** goods **3.** factories, depots **4.** sea-ports, airports, etc.

TASKS 4.4

Exercise 1

1. selling goods or services via the Internet **2.** They do not have to give part of their profits to intermediaries. **3.** the travel industry **4.** They can choose how and when to shop.

Exercise 2

1. cold calls **2.** online retail **3.** free samples **4.** direct mail

Exercise 3

B2B: 2, 4
B2C: 1, 3, 5, 6

TASKS 4.5

Exercise 1

a. checkout **b.** bar code **c.** point of sale **d.** retail outlet **e.** merchandising **f.** loyalty cards

Exercise 2

1, 3, 4, 5

Exercise 3

1. c **2.** d **3.** e **4.** b **5.** a

TASKS 5.1

Exercise 1

1. yes **2.** no **3.** yes

Exercise 2

a. 5 **b.** 1 **c.** 2 **d.** 4 **e.** 3

Exercise 3

1. CC Corporation **2.** HT Communications **3.** Vargon Ltd **4.** 2011

TASKS 5.2

Exercise 1

a. feedback **b.** praise **c.** complaints **d.** refund

Exercise 2

1. b **2.** c **3.** d **4.** a

Exercise 3

1. false **2.** true **3.** true **4.** false **5.** true **6.** false **7.** false

TASKS 5.3

Exercise 1

1. It allows you to log information about them. **2.** It lets you record, track, analyse, manage and synchronize orders. **3.** information **4.** information flow **5.** initiate, chase or make payments

Exercise 2

1. c **2.** e **3.** a **4.** d **5.** b

Exercise 3

1. b **2.** c **3.** a

TASKS 5.4

Exercise 1

a. reviews **b.** social media **c.** subjective **d.** negative **e.** recommend **f.** monitor

Exercise 2

1. P **2.** N **3.** P **4.** A **5.** N

Exercise 3

1. c **2.** a **3.** b

TASKS 5.5

Exercise 1

a. protection **b.** rights **c.** data

Exercise 2

1. d **2.** c **3.** a **4.** e **5.** b

Exercise 3

a. false **b.** false **c.** true **d.** true **e.** true **f.** true

TASKS 6.1

Exercise 1

a. human resources **b.** staff **c.** employee **d.** planning **e.** self-employed **f.** freelance

Exercise 2

Individual term: a, c, e
Collective term: b, d

Exercise 3

1. b **2.** a **3.** c

Exercise 4

a, b, d, f, g

TASKS 6.2

Exercise 1

1. f **2.** d **3.** g **4.** b **5.** e **6.** a **7.** c

Exercise 2

a. recruit/hire **b.** hire/recruit **c.** reference **d.** CV/résumé **e.** résumé/CV **f.** probationary

Exercise 3

1. trainee managers/management trainees (customer service) **2.** London **3.** sales and customer service **4.** Six months **5.** CV + reference

TASKS 6.3

Exercise 1

1. leave their job **2.** sack; fire **3.** the role is no longer necessary, or they can no longer afford to pay them **4.** payment of a lump sum of money or keeping a pension

Exercise 2

Employer: 1, 4, 7, 9
Employee: 2, 3, 5, 6, 8

Exercise 3

b. severance

TASKS 6.4

Exercise 1

a. remuneration **b.** payroll **c.** salary **d.** benefits **e.** bonuses **f.** performance-related **g.** share options **h.** pension

Exercise 2

1, 3, 5, 6, 7, 10

Exercise 3

2. Carolina

TASKS 6.5

Exercise 1

a. industrial relations **b.** staff representatives **c.** works council **d.** arbitration **e.** trade union **f.** strike **g.** industrial action **h.** grievance **i.** tribunal

Exercise 2

1. establish a works council **2.** proposed changes in working conditions **3.** recent and probable developments and activities; establishment's economic situation

Exercise 3

number of hours: c
type of employment: j, k
pay: g, h
benefits: a, b
disciplinary procedures: e
notice: d
grievance procedures: f
employee rights: i

TASKS 6.6

Exercise 1

a. disability **b.** equal opportunities **c.** positive action **d.** under-represented **e.** equal opportunities monitoring **f.** discriminated against

Exercise 2

1. a. decreased **b.** no **c.** yes **d.** black **e.** white
2. a. more women **b.** increased employment
c. more women

TASKS 7.1

Exercise 1

a. motivates **b.** supervised **c.** theory X **d.** responsibility **e.** theory Y **f.** motivated **g.** management consultants

Exercise 2

theory x: 2, 4
theory y: 1, 3

TASKS 7.2

Exercise 1

a. 3 **b.** 2 **c.** 1

Exercise 2

1. a, b **2.** b **3.** b, c

Exercise 3

1. their staff **2.** training needs of staff
3. monitor and review performance of staff
4. ensures that staff remain motivated

TASKS 7.3

Exercise 1

1. line manager **2.** report **3.** leadership **4.** organizing **5.** promotion

Exercise 2

hierarchical structure

Exercise 3

1. 3 **2.** 1 **3.** 2 **4.** 2 **5.** Line Manager D **6.** hierarchical

TASKS 7.4

Exercise 1

a. change management **b.** restructuring **c.** threatened **d.** reassure **e.** thrive **f.** consult **g.** stakeholders **h.** crisis management

Exercise 2

1. feels threatened by change **2.** thrives on change
3. thrives on change **4.** feels threatened by change

Exercise 3

1. c **2.** d **3.** a **4.** b

TASKS 8.1

Exercise 1

a. career path **b.** retraining **c.** skills **d.** drive **e.** networking **f.** contacts **g.** sideways

Exercise 2

1. at the beginning of your career **2.** at the end of your career/after you have retired **3.** to learn new skills **4.** a sideways move

Exercise 3

qualifications = e
employment = c
technical skills = a
personal skills = b

personal interests = d
references = f

TASKS 8.2

Exercise 1

a. first degree **b.** diploma **c.** MBA **d.** sponsored **e.** specialisms **f.** apprenticeships

Exercise 2

a. part-time **b.** full-time **c.** distance learning **d.** part-time **e.** distance learning

Exercise 3

1. c **2.** a **3.** d **4.** b

TASKS 8.3

Exercise 1

a. staff development **b.** in-house **c.** training **d.** workshop **e.** role plays **f.** case studies

Exercise 2

1. Using computers **2.** Health & Safety in the workplace **3.** Prioritizing / Time management **4.** Project management **5.** Dealing with conflict **6.** Presenting **7.** Negotiating

Exercise 3

True: 1, 3, 4, 5
False: 2, 6

TASKS 8.4

Exercise 1

a. asset **b.** mentor **c.** mentored **d.** mentee **e.** confidential **f.** coaching **g.** one-to-one **h.** facilitate

Exercise 2

1. c **2.** b **3.** a **4.** a

TASKS 8.5

Exercise 1

a. on leave **b.** holiday **c.** sick leave **d.** parental leave **e.** compassionate leave **f.** absenteeism **g.** stress **h.** sick building syndrome **i.** turnover

Exercise 2

a. Oyez Engineering, Breakers Inc. **b.** Daniel's Motor Co. **c.** Breakers Inc. **d.** Breakers Inc. **e.** Daniel's Motor Co.

Exercise 3

1. call in sick **2.** sick leave **3.** casual dress codes **4.** Monday

TASKS 9.1

Exercise 1

prices rising: boom, bull
prices falling: bust, bear

Exercise 2

a. boom **b.** slump **c.** boom-bust **d.** booming **e.** stock-market collapse

Exercise 3

a. no **b.** sold **c.** increase **d.** decrease **e.** yes

TASKS 9.2

Exercise 1

a. B **b.** D **c.** A **d.** G **e.** A **f.** C

Exercise 2

2. The price for Company A's shares was £2.05. This was an increase of 2.3%. Investors can expect to receive a yield of 9%.
3. The price for Company B's shares was £13.39. This was an increase of 1.4%. Investors can expect to receive a yield of 2.9%.
4. The price for Company C's shares was £1.81. This was a decrease of 0.9%. Investors cannot expect to receive any yield.
5. The price for Company E's shares was £3.66. This was a decrease of 1.6%. Investors can expect to receive a yield of 2.6%.
6. The price for Company F's shares was £3.75. This was a decrease of 1.4%. The yield figures are unavailable.
7. The price for Company G's shares was £1.80. This was a decrease of 3.4%. Investors can expect to receive a yield of 4.4%.

Exercise 3

a. stock exchange **b.** invest; investment **c.** bond **d.** bond **e.** investor

TASKS 9.3

Exercise 1

column 1: to increase, to improve, to reach a peak, to peak
column 2: to level off, to stabilize, to remain constant
column 3: to decrease, to fall, to drop

Exercise 2

1. levelled off **2.** increased gradually/improved steadily **3.** fell slightly **4.** increased gradually/improved steadily **5.** peaked dramatically **6.** remained constant **7.** grew rapidly/increased sharply **8.** grew rapidly/increased sharply

Exercise 3

1. increased **2.** temporary fall **3.** steadily

TASKS 9.4

Exercise 1

1, 2, 3, 7, 8

Exercise 2

a. true **b.** true **c.** false **d.** false

Exercise 3

a. The telecommunications industry is experiencing a downturn. **b.** After a downturn in the oil industry, there was a sudden spike in oil prices.

TASKS 9.5

Exercise 1

a. go out of business **b.** ailing **c.** turn it around **d.** troubleshooting **e.** going bankrupt

Exercise 2

1. c **2.** b **3.** d **4.** a **5.** e

Exercise 3

1. a **2.** c **3.** d **4.** b

Exercise 4

pleased: 3, 6
worried: 1, 2, 4, 5

TASKS 10.1

Exercise 1

a. gross **b.** profit margin **c.** mark-up **d.** profitability **e.** breaks even

Exercise 2

a. 1 **b.** 2 **c.** 5 **d.** 3 **e.** 4

Exercise 3

1. c **2.** a **3.** d **4.** b

TASKS 10.2

Exercise 1

a. maximize profit **b.** new markets **c.** growth in sales turnover **d.** expansion **e.** market share

Exercise 2

1. c **2.** e **3.** b **4.** a **5.** f **6.** d

Exercise 3

1. b **2.** d **3.** a **4.** c

Exercise 4

1. false **2.** true **3.** true

TASKS 10.3

Exercise 1

a. undercuts **b.** price wars **c.** predatory pricing **d.** collude **e.** price fixing **e.** cartel

Exercise 2

predatory pricing: the consumer
price wars: the consumer
price discrimination: the seller
cartels: the seller
loss leaders: the consumer

Exercise 3

1. loss leaders **2.** predatory pricing **3.** price discrimination **4.** price wars **5.** cartels

Exercise 4

1. b **2.** b

TASKS 10.4

Exercise 1

a. manufacturing base **b.** relocate
c. enterprise zones **d.** clusters **e.** synergies

Exercise 2

1. c **2.** a **3.** b **4.** d

Exercise 3

1. enterprise zone **2.** cluster **3.** brownfield site
4. greenfield site

TASKS 10.5

Exercise 1

1. worried **2.** moving the brand downmarket
3. to reposition the brand/appeal to discount shoppers **4.** It could damage the brand image with existing customers.

Exercise 2

moving the brand upmarket:
advantage: **d**
disadvantage: **a**

moving the brand downmarket:
advantage: **b**
disadvantage: **c**

Exercise 3

1. b **2.** a

Exercise 4

1. false **2.** true **3.** false **4.** true **5.** true
6. false

TASKS 11.1

Exercise 1

a. credit **b.** accounts receivable **c.** accounts payable **d.** invoices **e.** cash flow

Exercise 2

column 1: money owed to the company
column 2: money the company owes

Exercise 3

a, b

Exercise 4

1. get paid **2.** sell and expect to be paid
3. get closer to them **4.** your credit terms
5. issue proper invoices

Exercise 5

1. c **2.** a **3.** b

TASKS 11.2

Exercise 1

a. costs **b.** cost structures **c.** fixed costs
d. direct costs **e.** indirect costs **f.** overheads

Exercise 2

cost of producing goods: 1, 4
non-production costs: 2, 3

Exercise 3

2, 3, 4

Exercise 4

1. e **2.** a **3.** d **4.** b **5.** f **6.** c

Exercise 5

1. £112 000 (= insurance+equipment+rent)
2. £925 000 (= heating+wages+raw materials+canteen)

Exercise 6

1. true **2.** true **3.** false **4.** true **5.** true

TASKS 11.3

Exercise 1

profit and loss
asset and liability

Exercise 2

1. d **2.** c **3.** a **4.** e **5.** b **6.** f

Exercise 3

2, 3, 1

Exercise 4

a. results **b.** profit and loss account/balance sheet
c. profit and loss account/balance sheet
d. auditors **e.** assets **f.** liabilities **g.** interim

TASKS 11.4

Exercise 1

a. loan **b.** interest **c.** interest rates
d. overdraft **e.** debt

Exercise 2

1. Eva Co. Ltd. **2.** Delaware Inc.
3. Bright Brothers **4.** £50,000 **5.** Chris Ltd.

Exercise 3

high interest rates: a, b, e, f
low interest rates: c, d

TASKS 11.5

Exercise 1

a. 2 **b.** 3 **c.** 1 **d.** 5 **e.** 6 **f.** 4

Exercise 2

1. raise capital **2.** participate in a rights issue
3. share issue/flotation **4.** by arranging a bank loan

Exercise 3

a. takeover **b.** working capital **c.** liquidity
d. financing

TASKS 12.1

Exercise 1

1. firm **2.** commerce **3.** big business
4. corporations **5.** small businesses
6. start-ups

Exercise 2

List A: 1, 2, 3, 4, 6
List B: 5

Exercise 3

1. a corporation **2.** a large firm
3. small businesses

TASKS 12.2

Exercise 1

Backers: 1, 2, 4, 7, 8

Exercise 2

1. backers **2.** business plan **3.** breakeven
4. cash flow **5.** overheads **6.** budget

Exercise 3

a. 4 **b.** 2 **c.** 3 **d.** 5 **e.** 1 **f.** 6

TASKS 12.3

Exercise 1

Primary Sector: b, f, g, l, q
Secondary Sector: e, i, j, k, p, r
Tertiary Sector: a, c, d, h, m, n, o

Exercise 2

1. Country B **2.** Country C **3.** Country A

Exercise 3

a. industries **b.** private **c.** public **d.** productive
e. financial, service

TASKS 12.4

Exercise 1

Organizations that control another company: 1, 3
Companies whose shares are held by another company: 2, 4

Exercise 2

a. group **b.** holding company **c.** sister companies
d. associated companies

Exercise 3

a. a sole trader **b.** a plc **c.** a limited company
d. a franchise

TASKS 12.5

Exercise 1

a. consortium, joint venture **b.** expansion, grow the business **c.** acquisition, takeover
d. join forces, merge

Exercise 2

1. true **2.** false **3.** false **4.** true **5.** true
6. false **7.** false

Exercise 3

a. business strategy **b.** local partner
c. expansion strategy

Exercise 4

1. local partner **2.** takeover **3.** joint venture

TASKS 13.1

Exercise 1

a. hardware **b.** desktop **c.** laptop **d.** built-in
e. peripherals **f.** wireless **g.** smartphones
h. tablets **i.** touch-screens

Exercise 2

Computers: laptop, tablet, desktop
Peripherals: external speakers, camera, printer, headphones

Exercise 3

1. c **2.** a **3.** b **4.** c **5.** b **6.** a

TASKS 13.2

Exercise 1

a. install **b.** suite **c.** applications
d. open source **e.** word processing **f.** spreadsheet
g. upgrade **h.** software **i.** download

Exercise 2

1. c **2.** a **3.** d **4.** b

Exercise 3

1. d **2.** b **3.** e **4.** a **5.** c

TASKS 13.3

Exercise 1

a. business management software **b.** integrate
c. functions **d.** ERP **e.** site and user licences
f. external consultants **g.** specialist software

Exercise 2

1. d **2.** c **3.** b **4.** f **5.** a **6.** e

Exercise 3

business management software: 1, 4, 5, 7, 8, 10
external consultant: 2, 3, 6, 9

TASKS 13.4

Exercise 1

a. networks **b.** backed up **c.** storage
d. hard drive **e.** flash drive **f.** encrypting
g. LAN **h.** cloud computing

Exercise 2

1. WAN **2.** LAN **3.** VPN **4.** WLAN

Exercise 3

1. c **2.** a **3.** b

TASKS 13.5

Exercise 1

a. help desk **b.** passwords **c.** crashing
d. freezing **e.** hacking into **f.** viruses **g.** worms
h. spyware **i.** phishing

Exercise 2

1. freezing **2.** crashed, down **3.** phishing
4. virus **5.** password **6.** hacked

Exercise 3

a. true **b.** false **c.** true **d.** true **e.** true
f. false

TASKS 14.1

Exercise 1

a. free trade **b.** protectionism **c.** quotas
d. imports **e.** exports **f.** tariffs/customs duties
g. tariffs/customs duties

Exercise 2

1. b **2.** d **3.** f **4.** e **5.** a **6.** c

Exercise 3

1. e **2.** b **3.** d **4.** c **5.** a

TASKS 14.2

Exercise 1

1. d **2.** c **3.** g **4.** b **5.** a **6.** f **7.** e

Exercise 2

plus points: b, d, f
minus points: a, c, e, g

Exercise 3

1. true **2.** false **3.** true **4.** true **5.** false
6. false **7.** true

TASKS 14.3

Exercise 1

a. competitors **b.** compete **c.** competitive edge/ competitive advantage **d.** competitive edge/ competitive advantage **e.** key players **f.** monopolies

Exercise 2

1. b **2.** a **3.** d **4.** c

Exercise 3

1. Moto Swift **2.** Auto Vitesse, Airlie Rapide **3.** no **4.** Moto Swift **5.** Thomson Brio

Exercise 4

a. true **b.** false **c.** true **d.** true

TASKS 14.4

Exercise 1

a. balance of payments **b.** current account **c.** capital account **d.** trade deficit **e.** trade surplus **f.** exchange rate **g.** pegged **h.** visible **i.** invisible

Exercise 2

1. true **2.** false **3.** true **4.** false **5.** true

Exercise 3

visible imports: bananas, oil, cars, processed food, rice
invisible imports: tourism, insurance

Exercise 4

a. true **b.** false **c.** true **d.** true **e.** false

TASKS 15.1

Exercise 1

a. 1, 5, 6, 7 **b.** 2, 3, 4, 8 **c.** developing (1, 5, 6, 7)

Exercise 2

a, d, e, g, h

Exercise 3

Maya and Youssef

Exercise 4

1. false **2.** true **3.** false **4.** true **5.** false

TASKS 15.2

Exercise 1

a. fair trade **b.** developing **c.** producers and growers **d.** cash crops **e.** world market prices **f.** commodities **g.** Fairtrade mark **h.** fair trade

Exercise 2

free trade system: a, c, e
Fairtrade system: b, d, f

Exercise 3

1. Paulo **2.** low **3.** low **4.** higher **5.** Paulo

TASKS 15.3

Exercise 1

increase corporate social responsibility: d, e
barriers to corporate social responsibility: a, b, c

Exercise 2

a. corporate social responsibility **b.** social costs/ social benefits **c.** social costs/social benefits **d.** social audit **e.** mission statement

Exercise 3

1. c **2.** a **3.** d **4.** b

Exercise 4

1. yes **2.** yes **3.** no **4.** yes

TASKS 15.4

Exercise 1

1. flexitime **2.** homeworker **3.** job sharing **4.** hot-desking **5.** part-time

Exercise 2

1. true **2.** false **3.** true **4.** false **5.** true **6.** true

Exercise 3

company: smaller premises, wider choice of potential employees, lower overheads
employee: no commuting, flexible working hours, no restrictions on where you live

Index

The numbers refer to the topic numbers.

DUDLEY COLLEGE
LIBRARY